STARTUP

IDEA

SHAKER

STARTUP IDEA SHAKER

DUAL FRAMEWORK APPROACH FOR GENERATING, REFINING AND VALIDATING IDEAS

Puneet Suri

For My Mother, Whose Unwavering Confidence
In Me Inspires Me To Keep Moving Forward
Every Day.

Contents

Preface 9

Introduction 13

Part 1: The Idea Shaker Framework............... 17

Introduction: Part 1 19

Chapter 1: The Power Law and What It Means For Founders 21

Chapter 2: The "Idea Shaker" Framework 27

Part 2: Develop a Working Model of Your Startup... 45

Introduction: Part 2 47

Chapter 3: Develop a Working Model of Your Idea 49

Foundational Tool 1: Profit Pools 53

Foundational Tool 2: Revenue Models 61

Foundational Tool 3: Competitor Analysis 71

Part 3: The VIBE Framework 77

Introduction: Part 3 79

Chapter 4: Validating the Idea - Testing Before the Leap 85

Chapter 5: Identifying Market Size 101

Chapter 6: Building Differentiation 111

Chapter 7: Establishing Economics........123

Part 4: Practical Guidelines on the VC process
.... 139

Introduction: Part 4 141

Chapter 8: Planning Your Startup's Funding Requirements 143

Chapter 9: Valuation.............................. 149

Chapter 10: Approaching the Funding Journey.. 153

Chapter 11: Crafting Your Pitch Deck .. 155

Chapter 12: Building a Financial Model 159

Preface

I entered the investing world in 2006 after ten years in management consulting - 6 years with Ernst & Young and shorter stints with Kearney and KSA. The consulting world thrives on standardized frameworks for analysis and decision-making; structures bring efficiency to thinking, clear mental clutter, and guide decision-making.

However, the investing world was different - each individual had a unique approach based on his background. Most venture capital (VC) and private equity (PE) professionals came from two camps: ex-management consultants or ex-investment bankers. The latter group leaned heavily on financial modeling, but when it comes to early-stage investing, financial models offer little value. At this stage, the numbers are hypothetical at best - of course, basic unit economics must be analyzed to assess whether a startup would turn profitable, but beyond that, much of the evaluation relies on qualitative judgment, a keen understanding of the market and the founder's vision.

What also intrigued me a lot as an investor was the diversity of complexities that founders faced:

Some founders had brilliant startup ideas - ones we would later see succeed spectacularly- but they struggled early on to articulate why their ideas would work. They found it challenging to express their intuition in concrete terms or to communicate effectively to investors.

At the same time, I met industry experts eager to embark on their entrepreneurial journey but unsure how to proceed. They lacked an approach to identify and validate ideas, leaving them in a constant state of analysis paralysis.

Then there were founders who launched startups with ideas that made no economic sense. It was disheartening to see so much time, effort, and hope poured into ventures that might have been abandoned early on had they been viewed through an outcome oriented lens.

Equally, I encountered many "want-to-be founders" who, due to personal circumstances, were better off continuing their salaried jobs instead of venturing into the uncertainties of a startup life.

For years, these interactions with founders left me with a nagging discomfort: the absence of a structured approach to shape their thought processes. Writing this book has been a cathartic experience - a way to address that discomfort by providing a method for generating, evaluating, and validating startup ideas.

Whether you're trying to find the right idea, refine an existing one, or ensure its viability, my sincere hope is that this book will serve as a practical guide, helping you move forward with clarity and purpose.

While my experience is rooted largely in the Indian startup ecosystem, the frameworks and strategies in this book are designed to apply to founders, investors, and professionals across geographies. The principles of clarity, validation, and structured thinking transcend markets, making this book relevant for anyone on an entrepreneurial or investment journey anywhere in the world.

Introduction

The purpose of this book is to serve as a practical toolkit for generating, validating, and refining startup ideas. The book is divided into four parts:

Part 1: The "Idea Shaker"
This part introduces the unique and simple Idea Shaker, built around three key axes:
1. Product Type
2. Catalyst
3. Consumer Awareness

This framework can be used in two powerful ways:
1. **Shake, validate, and refine an early idea**: This preliminary analysis helps you decide whether an idea is worth exploring further or if it should be abandoned early, saving time and resources.
2. **Generate ideas**: If you're an industry expert exploring startup opportunities, the framework allows you to systematically create ideas by selecting positions in the matrix.

The ideas that pass through this filter can then be evaluated further using the framework in Parts 2 and 3.

Part 2: Develop a "Working Model" of Your Idea

A Working Model is a structured (yet flexible) plan that defines how your idea will solve a problem, deliver value to the customer, and generate revenue. It serves as the first draft of your startup's foundation, which will later be validated, tested, and refined through Part 3 of this book (the VIBE Framework).

Part 2 will also briefly touch upon three very useful business analysis frameworks:

1. Profit Pools
2. Revenue Models
3. Competitor Analysis

Part 3: The VIBE Framework

Once you've shortlisted ideas using the Shaker and developed them in Part 2, Part 3 provides the **VIBE Framework** to evaluate them in-depth and finalize them. This iterative framework comprises four essential elements:

- **<u>V</u>alidation**: Confirming demand and customer interest

- **<u>I</u>dentifying Market Size**: Estimating potential opportunities

- **<u>B</u>uilding Differentiation**: Establishing competitive advantages and moats

- **<u>E</u>stablishing Economics**: Understanding financial viability and scalability – unit economics, lifetime value, contribution margins, etc.

The VIBE Framework is designed to be used iteratively as you refine your idea. By the end of this process, you will have evaluated your startup idea with the rigor of a venture capitalist.

Part 4: Practical Guidelines

The final section provides practical guidelines on:

1. Approaching the funding journey
2. Valuation Considerations
3. Crafting an impactful pitch deck
4. Developing a financial model that appeals to investors

This section ensures you can articulate your business idea effectively and present it in a way that resonates with potential investors and other stakeholders.

Who This Book Is For

This book is for anyone looking to approach startup creation systematically:

1. Aspiring founders seeking clarity in generating and validating their ideas
2. Professionals transitioning into entrepreneurship who need a structured approach to develop their first startup idea

3. Early-stage investors or VCs who want a framework to analyze startups and guide founders.
4. Corporate leaders exploring intrapreneurship or innovation initiatives within their organizations.

The unique frameworks outlined in this book - The Idea Shaker and VIBE - are designed to address the core principles of startup creation. These principles are not bound by geography or industry rather apply universally.

How to Use This Book

It's ideal to read the book sequentially on your first pass, starting with Part 1 and progressing through to Part 4. This will give you a holistic understanding of the startup journey, from ideation to execution.

Once you've familiarized yourself with the frameworks, revisit specific chapters for deeper insights.

Every startup journey is different. The frameworks in this book are designed to be flexible, allowing you to adapt them to your industry, market, and personal situation. While this isn't a guaranteed formula for success, it offers practical tools to help you think more clearly, ask the right questions, and approach your ideas with greater confidence and structure.

Part 1: The Idea Shaker Framework

Introduction: Part 1

Chapter 1 of the book explains "The Power Law," its impact on startup outcomes, and how it shapes the founder's journey.

Chapter 2 introduces the "Idea Shaker" Framework. This chapter explains the construct of the Shaker and how to use it in the following two ways:

1. Deconstruct an idea into its essential components in order to validate it
2. Generate a startup idea if you have an understanding of a sector

Chapter 1: The Power Law and What It Means For Founders

If you are going to be a part of the startup ecosystem, I would like to begin with an interesting concept: **"The Power Law"**, and highlight its implications for founders.

As an investor, I am acutely aware of the Power Law. It is often used in the context of creating a startup portfolio by investors to emphasize the risks associated with startups.

So, what is the Power Law? The Power Law is a phenomenon that appears across nature, society, and economics. Essentially, it describes situations where a small number of players account for a disproportionately large share of the output in their system. For example, in nature, a handful of species account for the majority of biomass. In human society, wealth distribution follows the Power Law pattern: a small percentage of people control a large share of wealth. Cities also reflect this pattern, with a few large metropolitan areas hosting most of the population, while countless smaller towns are sparsely populated. The Power Law phenomena can be observed in social networks, where a few platforms attract most users, and in the context of online content, where a few viral posts capture the majority of attention.

In the startup context, the Power Law implies that only a very few startups will generate nearly all the success and wealth in the ecosystem. This pattern, where a small number of startups create most of the wealth, consistently emerges regardless of how much analysis goes into investment decisions. While initial due diligence aims to identify companies with potential, it can only assess visible factors at the time. However, market dynamics, customer adoption, regulations, and other factors over a period of time play pivotal roles in determining whether a company eventually succeeds or fails. No matter how promising the idea initially appears, most startups will fall short of achieving massive returns, while a few will exceed all expectations. The exceptional startups will grow exponentially (not linearly) and dominate their market segments, often creating returns that dwarf initial projections.

Recognizing this, investors focus on identifying those rare opportunities that can yield outsized returns, understanding that most of their portfolio is likely to fail to provide any meaningful returns. In the startup world, the Power Law serves as a constant reminder that a few exceptional startups—often unpredictable at the outset—will generate the majority of returns.

Venture capitalists (VCs) therefore diversify their portfolios and limit their investments in any single startup to a certain percentage. In India, VC funds must register with the regulator SEBI, which restricts the maximum investment in a single company to between 10% and 25%, depending on the type of fund.

Now the question is: how does this affect you as a founder?

Unlike a VC firm, as a founder you cannot diversify your risk - you are committed to one startup, which is your own. The implications are significant for you as a founder. Regardless of how confident you are in your own idea, you are bound by the realities of the Power Law—there is no escaping it.

The question is: Are you in a position to take the risk and pursue the chance of generating extreme returns as a founder?

How do you decide? You consider the following three points.

Firstly, determine whether you are in a position to take the plunge. Do you have the financial cushion? I'm not here to throw around numbers, but you need to evaluate various factors:

- Savings and investments
- Mortgages and liabilities
- Stage of life—family responsibilities

You will receive significant equity in your startup in lieu of your regular monthly salary. You may also take a salary, but it will likely be a fraction of your market salary. Your equity is illiquid and could be worth nothing if the startup doesn't succeed. Can you take that risk? This also largely depends on the next question.

Secondly consider whether you have "profile security." Simply put, if the startup fails, will your experience be seen as valuable, or as merely an attempt to create a job for yourself when no one else was offering you one? Only you can judge, but your failed startup should not come across as disguised unemployment. Trust me, I receive many startup pitches each month, and a significant percentage are simply attempts to keep busy due to a lack of proper employment opportunities for the founders.

Less than 2% of startups receive funding, and it's a fact that pedigree matters when seeking investment. Among unicorn startups in India, 50% of the founders are from IITs.

Finally, do you have the passion and strength to run your startup for years in pursuit of success while your peers buy houses, cars, and settle down? Only you can answer that.

The objective here is not to discourage you from pursuing your idea, but rather to ensure you enter the world of startups with your eyes wide open. Founding a startup is exhilarating, but it's also a high-stakes endeavor.

Once you have decided to take the plunge, how do you maximize your chances of success? You do your full homework before jumping in, and that's where this book comes in.

This book will guide you in two crucial ways: first, to carry out "idea-shaking" that helps you identify ideas worth pursuing; and second, to understand the steps needed to develop and critically evaluate that idea once you've identified it.

In the next chapter, we will begin with the *Idea Shaker*, which will help you systematically break down and assess potential ideas. This framework is designed to enable you to evaluate your ideas against practical criteria, allowing you to focus your energy on the most promising opportunities.

Chapter 2: The "Idea Shaker" Framework

Before introducing the "Idea Shaker," it's important to take a step back and examine what establishes a solid foundation for a successful startup. Entrepreneurship is a demanding journey, filled with highs and lows that test a founder's resilience, adaptability, and commitment.

The Skill-Gap-Passion Nexus: Successful businesses consistently emerge at the intersection of three crucial factors:

1- Hard skills of founders

2- Market gaps

3- Personality and passions of the founders

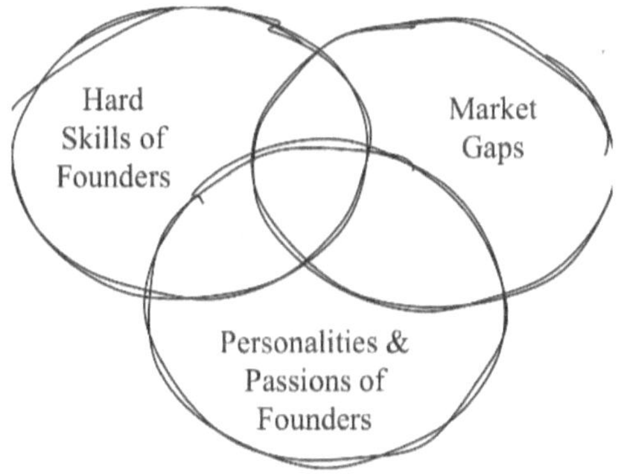

Each of these factors is individually important, but what is most relevant is that the idea should lie at their intersection.

At this intersection, these factors come together to create a powerful nexus that maximizes the chances of success.

Hard Skills of Founders

The technical expertise and specialized knowledge that founders bring to the table provide the backbone for creating a sustainable and long-lasting business. Hard skills can include anything from product design and engineering to finance, operations, and sales. Each founder's unique skill set allows him to navigate the complexities of their industry and address challenges efficiently.

For example, a founder with a software engineering background can iterate on a SAAS product rapidly, incorporating customer feedback without needing to rely extensively on an outside development team. Similarly, a founder with a background in finance can manage cash flows more effectively or negotiate financial terms with investors. This proficiency ensures that decisions are made quickly and with a depth of understanding that keeps the business agile and on track.

Moreover, possessing these skills builds confidence with investors, employees, and customers. A technically proficient founder can instill trust, signaling to stakeholders that he understands the industry and has the capability to execute. Without these hard skills, the business may be more dependent on outside expertise and may struggle to make quick adjustments in its journey toward success. In essence, these competencies are the foundational tools that turn an idea into a viable, functioning business.

Identifying Market Gaps

Market gaps represent unmet needs, underserved customer segments, or pain points that current players in the market have overlooked or are unable to address due to their legacy processes, historical brand positioning, or cost structures. Identifying and understanding these gaps allows founders to tackle real issues that customers face.

Market gaps can be identified through rigorous research, competitor analysis, or even personal experiences that reveal industry shortcomings. Founders with a deep understanding of a specific industry can often spot these gaps easily. For example, the rise of fintech startups in recent years was largely driven by traditional financial institutions' failure to serve tech-savvy consumers who demanded more accessible, mobile-friendly solutions. By recognizing this need, startups like Paytm and

Stripe capitalized on the opportunity to provide differentiated services.

Recognizing a market gap also involves understanding what potential customers are looking for but may not yet be articulating. Sometimes this entails creating an entirely new category, as Airbnb did with the concept of shared, short-term lodging. Other times, it involves addressing inefficiencies within existing categories, as seen with logistics startups that optimized delivery processes for e-commerce. Identifying these gaps empowers founders to create impactful, differentiated products that resonate, gain traction, and ultimately disrupt their sectors.

Personality and Passion of the Founders

The intrinsic motivation, personal drive, and alignment of interests of the founders are the underlying fuel that powers the journey from an idea in the mind to a profit-generating business. Passion drives founders to persevere despite setbacks, while personality influences how they build and lead their teams, interact with customers, and shape the company's culture.

Passion often translates into:

1. An energy that inspires employees and earns the trust of customers.

2. Resilience—a critical trait for entrepreneurs navigating the ups and downs of building a business.

The founder's personality also shapes the tone of the organization and influences the company's brand identity. For instance, a founder who values transparency and open communication is likely to build a company culture that prioritizes these values, creating a more cohesive and engaged team. A founder who is highly creative and risk-tolerant might instill an innovative, experimental approach that encourages rapid iteration and adaptability.

The alignment between personal interests and the business venture can be especially important in industries that demand authenticity, such as sustainable products or wellness services. A founder who is genuinely committed to sustainability, for example, will resonate more deeply with eco-conscious customers, attracting loyal supporters who share similar values. This authenticity helps the business connect with its audience on a personal level, building brand loyalty that is difficult for competitors to replicate.

The Power of Intersection

When these three aspects - hard skills, market gaps, and the founders' personality and passion - come together, they create a strong foundation for a successful startup. Each element reinforces the others. For instance, technical expertise enables rapid product development, which, when applied to a genuine market need, results in solutions that resonate with customers. Meanwhile, the founder's passion sustains their efforts through challenges and helps craft a compelling narrative that attracts both customers and investors.

Importantly, this intersection aligns with how investors evaluate startups and their teams. Startups operating at this intersection are more likely to catch an investor's eye.

This alignment acts as an initial filter. Many ideas may seem tempting, but if they don't match the founder's skills, address a real market gap, or ignite their personal drive, they're less likely to succeed long-term. By focusing on ideas where these three circles overlap, founders can eliminate distractions and direct their energy toward opportunities with genuine potential.

Now, let us move to the Idea Shaker Framework.

Startup Ideas: Serendipity is a Myth

In movies and bestselling books, founders often stumble upon breakthrough ideas by chance - a casual observation or a "eureka" moment. In reality, most successful founders don't rely on luck. They actively seek ideas and think objectively and dispassionately about them. This is where the **Idea Shaker** Framework introduced in this book comes into play. Over the years, I've seen countless startup ideas flourish into unicorns, and in hindsight, they all shared fundamental traits. The **Idea Shaker** is based on these traits.

The framework is not about providing definitive validation for your startup idea; it's about breaking down your idea into core components to help you understand its complexity, strengths, and challenges. This process allows you to see how well your idea aligns with your skills, resources, and ambitions. It also helps you compare multiple ideas and decide which one suits you best.

Whether you're starting with an idea or exploring opportunities in a specific industry, the framework works in both scenarios:

1. **Validating Existing Ideas**: The framework acts as a "shaker" to test ideas for top-level viability and maps them out.

2. **Generating New Ideas**: If you're exploring a specific industry, the framework helps create ideas where potential is inherent in their creation.

Let us look at the framework now, and then we shall examine some examples of how to use it.

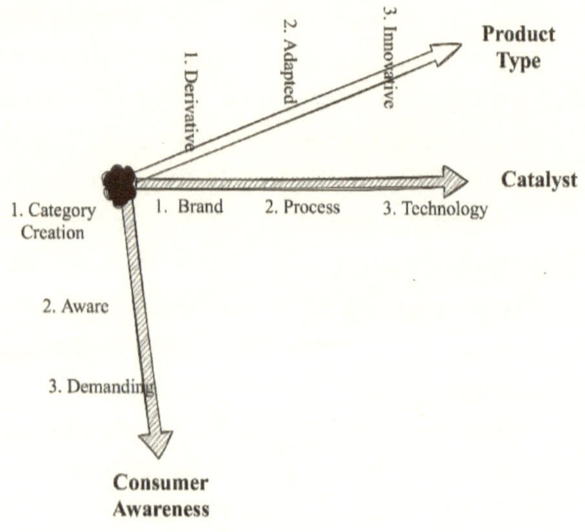

The Idea Shaker

The framework is built around three axes:

1. **Product Type**: Whether the product is a derivative (of an existing product), an adaptation (of an existing product), or an innovation.

2. **Consumer Awareness**: Whether customers are unaware (which entails category creation), aware, or demanding the product.

3. **Catalyst**: Whether the driving force behind the startup is brand, process, or technology.

Now, let us get into the details of each axis.

Product Type: This categorizes the product (or service) of the startup into one of the following three categories:

1.   **Derivative**: These are products that make incremental changes to existing offerings without fundamentally altering their core purpose or function. They rely on an established concept and compete mainly on minor variations such as aesthetics, packaging, or some functional upgrades. The stronger derivative models can target a new customer segment. Rapido can be considered a derivative of OLA Auto, as it focuses on two-wheeler taxis, providing a cheaper and faster alternative for solo travelers, particularly in congested city areas and smaller towns.

2.   **Adapted**: These products take an existing concept and modify it to better suit a specific market, audience, need, cultural differences. The changes are meaningful and designed to add new value or improve relevance. Derivative products copy with minimal innovation, while adapted products reinterpret or enhance an idea to solve a problem more effectively or appeal to a new audience. Urban Company can be considered an adaptation of Justdial, as Urban Company refined the model by integrating quality checks, fixed pricing, and direct bookings

through an app for home services like cleaning, plumbing, and beauty treatments.

3. **Innovative**: This is the strongest product type - products that redefine existing paradigms or create entirely new categories. They often have the potential to dominate markets, generate outsized returns, and set trends. This remains a compelling product category for a startup. For example, OLA was an innovation in India, even though it is a derivative of UBER. Similarly, Flipkart was a copy or a derivative of Amazon when it was launched in India but represented innovation in the context of the Indian market.

Consumer Awareness: This axis indicates how aware consumers are of their need for the startup's product or service.

1. **Consumer Unaware:** Consumers aren't aware of this need because it's a new concept. The startup is creating something entirely novel, necessitating the creation of a new category. Airbnb is a prime example, as it established the home-sharing category. Another example is Zomato Hyperpure, a B2B offering supplying fresh, high-quality ingredients to restaurants. The idea of a dedicated supply chain for restaurants was novel in India.

2. **Consumer Aware:** Consumers recognize this need but aren't actively seeking a solution.

They may believe a solution is not possible; this scenario indicates latent demand. While you may still need to market the product and educate the customer, you will require fewer resources than in category creation. When OLA launched in India, consumers were familiar with ride-hailing services due to UBER's presence in the USA. OLA leveraged this consumer awareness to enter the Indian market, incorporating India-specific customizations, such as accepting cash payments.

3. **Consumer Demanding:** Consumers are actively looking for solutions, indicating proven demand. This position is the easiest from the consumer awareness perspective. Razorpay entered the market as businesses sought better digital payment gateways to accommodate India's UPI boom. Razorpay addressed an already vocal demand for seamless payment integration.

This axis essentially captures the type of demand that exists for the startup's products: easy, expensive, or risky. Risky demand implies category creation, while easy demand exists when there is evidence that the customer is actively seeking the product. Expensive demand, on the other hand, arises when there is latent demand that must be converted into real demand.

Catalyst: In the Shaker, the catalyst represents the dominant competitive edge behind the idea and defines how you can differentiate your product from the competition. All consumer startups will have brand as a catalyst. In fact, all startups will incorporate all three catalysts to some degree. However, for this framework, the catalyst is the one that ultimately provides value to the customer. For example, there could be underlying processes that work behind the scenes to enable low prices in discounted store brands, or there could be a massive technology play providing services, as seen with OLA or UBER.

1. **Brand:** Brand as a catalyst implies that the key differentiator is the brand itself and that the product is more or less the same as that of the competition. It is generally a weak catalyst because the fundamental premise that any brand offers (quality and consistency) has become universal. Even established consumer brands were developed based on superior product attributes, processes, or technology.

There are two exceptions:

a. Introducing branded products in an unbranded category.

b. A legacy defunct brand (with strong recall and specific associations) is acquired and then relaunched to leverage the existing brand recognition. SAIC in China acquired MG (Morris Garage) and relaunched the car brand, while Reliance in India acquired the Campa Cola brand as two examples.

2. **Process:** Differentiation through a unique way of delivering or producing the product or offering superior value to the customer. For example, all low-priced retail brands utilize processes (with technology as an enabler) as the catalyst. The final low price to the customer is the outcome of a complex supply chain designed for extreme optimization.

3. **Technology:** Differentiation through technology can occur in two ways—technology as an enabler or technology as a core. Furthermore, it can be proprietary technology or widely available technology. Proprietary technology as a core to the product serves as a very strong catalyst. Facebook, for example, leveraged its technological prowess (algorithms) to become the omnipresent social media platform. Another example is ChatGPT, which has a 70% market share in the AI market. Non-proprietary technology can also serve as a strong catalyst, providing the startup with the runway to create a brand or establish itself with a loyal customer base before competition catches up.

How to Shape Your Idea Using This Framework:

Map your idea onto the three axes—Product, Consumer Awareness, and Catalyst. In each of the three axes, the value closest to the intersection is 1, and the furthest away is 3. Look at the picture of the Idea Shaker and its three axes at the beginning of this chapter. Write down the value combination for your startup.

Theoretically, there can be 27 combinations, but not all combinations in the matrix are logical. For example, if you have a derivative product with brand as a catalyst, it's not possible for customers to be unaware.

A value combination of 3-3-3 - indicating a "demanding" customer for an "innovative" product with "technology" as a catalyst - is very strong. This is a compelling proposition because there is demand for a product with no competition in the market, which is also difficult for competitors to replicate due to proprietary technology. Investors typically look for such opportunities that combine high consumer demand (or a clearly latent demand), a unique or innovative product, and a strong differentiator like technology.

Conversely, the combination of 1-2-1 for a derivative product targeting an aware customer with brand as the main catalyst is weak. This position can be easily copied by an incumbent or even by a newcomer. Equally, an incremental improvement may not excite investors, even if it is consumer-driven and maybe profitable in the short term.

Ideally, there should be at least one "3" or two "2"s in the value combination of your startup idea to have a decent chance of success. As an investor,

I generally look for a minimum total score (the sum of the individual combination values) of 5 to proceed with a detailed evaluation. A minimum score of 5 can be achieved with either two 2s or one 3, indicating that the idea can be evaluated further.

It is important to reiterate that the Idea Shaker is not about providing definitive validation for your startup idea—it's about breaking down your idea into core components to help you understand its complexity, strengths, and challenges.

Very importantly, the process allows you to see how well your idea aligns with your skills, resources, and ambitions. By analyzing your idea across these axes, you gain clarity on:

1. How difficult or resource-intensive it will be to execute

2. Whether your current skills match the needs of the idea

3. If you require additional resources, such as a co-founder with complementary skills (e.g., a marketer for category creation or a tech lead for an innovative product)

If you're exploring multiple opportunities, the Idea Shaker helps you compare them systematically. By evaluating ideas along three axes, you can prioritize those that are more feasible. This top-level filtering allows you to set aside ideas that don't meet basic criteria, focusing your time and resources on ideas with a higher likelihood of success. Once you have ideas that align well on all three fronts, you can move forward with a detailed analysis to evaluate them fully.

If you're from the industry, this framework is especially powerful. You already have insights into what's viable or what is too costly to develop and a sense of what trends investors might be excited about. The framework helps you leverage that industry expertise systematically. For instance, if you spot an idea that meets real consumer demand (rather than creating something no one knows they need), is an easy technology adaptation of an existing product, you instantly recognize it as having a solid foundation to pursue further. On the other hand, if an idea demands complex tech development with minimal consumer awareness, you know right away that it might be a harder sell, allowing you to move on without overthinking it.

How to Use the Idea Shaking Framework for Generating Ideas

If you looking to generate ideas in a specific industry, you can think through the combination of values on the axes. Let us look at the following hypothetical scenario:

1. Let's say you are a technologist in consumer products and you want to become an entrepreneur.

2. You don't have much exposure to the marketing function, and you don't want a co-founder either—so category creation is difficult. You must therefore focus on products that have demanding or at least strongly aware consumers.

3. From your experience in the industry, you know that many customers are interested in sustainable home goods, and as a technologist, you can create these "adapted" products that are differentiated from what is currently available in the market. These products are not "innovative" because they can be replicated.

4. However, you also realize that incumbent companies can launch sustainable products if your demand picks up. So, you need another differentiator. Moving along the catalyst axis, you choose to leverage "process' as a catalyst and launch your products with a subscription model. Since you are designing your supply chain from scratch, you can set up your processes accordingly, but it's difficult for incumbents to modify their systems.

5. You plan to evaluate sustainable cleaning supplies with a subscription model; the score on the Idea Shaker is 6.

Rather than letting ideas pass by untested or feeling the need to dive into deep research on each one, the framework encourages a top-level assessment. This first-pass analysis allows you to confidently discard weak ideas while keeping strong ones in focus. Ultimately, this structured approach is a tool to amplify your instincts, guiding you to better ideas and helping you avoid the trap of spreading your focus too thin.

An idea is just the beginning. To turn it into a viable startup, you need to develop a working model, which is your startup's foundation. In Part 2, we will develop a working model of the startup idea, which will then be evaluated and refined in Part 3—the VIBE framework.

Part 2: Develop a Working Model of Your Startup

Introduction: Part 2

This part of the book connects the early idea in Part 1 to the rigorous evaluation process in Part 3, specifically the VIBE framework, by developing a Working Model. A Working Model outlines the following:

1. The problem you're solving
2. Target customers
3. Value delivery and capture
4. Competitive positioning
5. A preliminary sense of financial viability (financial analysis relevant to an early-stage startup will be carried out as part of the VIBE framework)

This section also briefly explains three supporting frameworks—Profit Pools, Competitor Analysis, and Revenue Models. Although these frameworks were developed decades ago for traditional businesses, they are also relevant for startups. They can assist you in developing the working model and will be useful in applying the VIBE framework in Part 3 of the book.

Chapter 3: Develop a Working Model of Your Idea

Part 1 of this book has focused on exploration and ideation. You've examined whether entrepreneurship aligns with your life circumstances. You've also used the Idea Shaker to refine your idea and analyzed its core components to see if they align with your aspirations, strengths, and skills.

Now, as you stand at the threshold of evaluating your startup in detail, it's essential to define and articulate your idea in clearer, more tangible, and practical terms.

You are going to develop your idea into a working model - a draft blueprint that outlines how your startup will solve a specific problem, deliver value, and generate revenue and profits. This working model is not your final plan. Think of it as a foundation-in-progress that captures the essence of your idea while allowing for flexibility. It serves as your startup's first structure, to be refined through validation and testing in the VIBE Framework. This stage is crucial for refining your own thought process as well.

A Working Model shall cover the aspects as depicted in the diagram below.

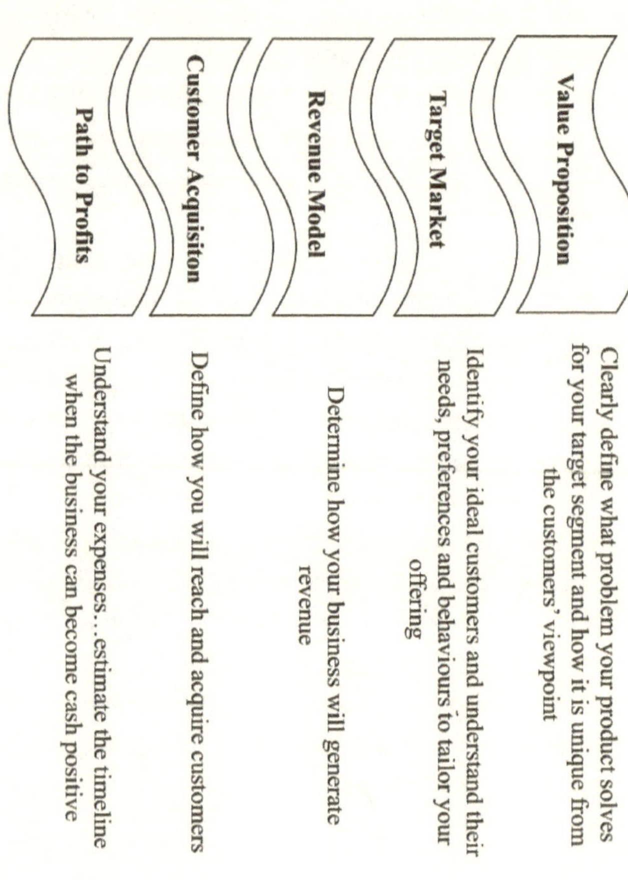

Elements of a Working Model

Each of these elements are now known in better clarity after the idea has passed through the Idea Shaker. You should also revisit three foundational tools given in the later part of this chapter: Profit Pools, Revenue Models, and Competitor Analysis.

These traditional frameworks, developed for established businesses, remain highly relevant for startups and will also play a role in the VIBE Framework (Part 3 of the book). For example, understanding profit pools helps in evaluating financial viability, and competitor analysis offers ideas to strengthen differentiation.

At the Working Model stage, Path to Profits means the plan as to how the business will eventually make money. The unit economics and contribution margins related concepts are explained in Part 3 of the book but at this stage the intent is to do a top level analysis on pricing, recurring costs, investment in developing the product, and get an idea regarding the time it will take to break even. Obvious factors that could indicate challenges in achieving profitability eventually need to be identified at this stage.

If you are unable to decide on a single option, it's fine to list two or more options and finalize them in the VIBE Framework instead.

Now it's time to put it all together in a clear, concise document that defines your startup idea. It must be specific enough to serve as a reference point as you progress through the next phases.

Why Write It Down?

Writing down your working model forces you to think critically. More importantly, it creates a tangible record of your thought process. This is helpful not just for you but also for potential investors and team members. You can reflect on this document as you validate, test, and refine your business idea further.

Writing it down also allows you to identify gaps. Think of this document as the blueprint that connects your raw idea to market the reality.

Let's next go through the three foundational tools which shall assist you in detailing out the Working Model of your startup.

Foundational Tool 1: Profit Pools

A profit pool can be defined as the sum total of all profits earned within an industry along the value chain of that industry. Although the concept is simple, the structure of a profit pool is generally complex. Profits will be deeper in some parts of the value chain than in others, and in addition, depth will vary within different customer segments as well. Segment profitability may vary widely by customer group, geographic market, or distribution channel. Profit pool analysis involves understanding the value chain points (as well as customer segments within) that are more profitable than others.

Different parts within an industry may have drastically different levels of profitability, and areas that generate the most revenue can sometimes have low margins. The goal of profit pool analysis is to help you determine whether you are focusing on the profitable parts of the industry.

The analysis can be quite straightforward and intuitive in many industries, but it can also be an eye-opener in others.

Identifying and tapping into startup opportunities in profitable segments can significantly impact long-term sustainability. Here's why:

- **Avoiding Low-Margin Pitfalls**: Without analyzing profit pools, startups may target segments that appear lucrative in terms of revenue but are actually low-margin. This could lead to unsustainable business models, where you generate revenue but struggle to achieve profitability.

- **Focusing Resources**: In the early stages of your startup, you don't have the luxury of endless resources to experiment. Knowing where the money is made helps you prioritize where to invest your time, effort, and capital.

- **Sustainability and Long-Term Growth**: Profit pools often provide resilient and repeatable sources of income. Focusing on high-margin segments ensures that your company can weather economic downturns, competition, or market changes. Patterns in profit pools change infrequently, and their structure can last for decades unless the startup itself is the disruptor.

Mapping Profit Pools: Examples across Industries

Here's how profit pool analysis works in some common industries:

Automotive Industry:

- **Revenue vs. Profit**: The majority of revenue in the automotive industry comes from vehicle sales. However, this is almost always a low-margin business due to the high costs of development, manufacturing, distribution, and competition.

- **After-Market and repair Services**: Maintenance services, spare parts, financing, and warranty programs offer higher profit margins, with some companies earning more from repairs than from actual vehicle sales.

- **Emerging Profit Pools**: With the rise of electric vehicles (EVs), profit pools are shifting toward technology ownership, battery production, charging infrastructure, and software-based services like autonomous driving technology. EV players have capitalized on this shift and are disrupting the traditional models of making profits.

Airline Industry:

There's a common phrase in the business world: "In the airline industry, everyone makes money except the airline." This sums up the importance of conducting profit pool analysis.

- **Economy Class**: While economy class tickets represent the majority of passengers, they don't generate large profits due to high operational costs, especially fuel costs.

- **Premium Services**: Business and first-class tickets generate much higher profits per passenger. Despite being a smaller share of total passengers, these customers contribute disproportionately to airline profits.

- **Ancillary Revenue**: Ancillary services like baggage fees, seat selection, food and beverage sales, and even in-flight entertainment generate higher margins than ticket sales. Ryanair generates about 30% of its revenue from these ancillary services, which helps offset the low margins from ticket sales.

- **Cargo**: Airlines also benefit from air freight, which is often a more stable and profitable source of income than passenger services, especially during economic downturns. Lufthansa Cargo and FedEx have capitalized on this segment.

Pointers on How to Do Profit Pool Analysis:

1. Understand the Value Chain of Your Industry

Break down your industry into its main components: production, distribution, sales, and after-sales services. Create a simple flowchart that shows where value is added and where costs are incurred.

2. Research Publicly Available Industry Reports

Utilize free sources such as government reports, trade publications, and industry blogs. Look for reports that discuss margins in your sector. For instance, industry associations often publish data on segment profitability. Reports by FICCI or NASSCOM in India frequently highlight profitable segments in several industries.

3. Analyze Competitors' Financials

For public companies, review financial statements and investor presentations to identify which segments contribute the most to revenue and profits. For example, Paytm's financial disclosures reveal where it earns revenue (such as payments, lending, and commerce) and the profitability of each vertical.

4. Use Proxy Benchmarks for Private Companies

If direct data isn't available, seek proxies or analogous companies in similar industries or markets. Study how a comparable startup in another country allocates resources and generates profits. For instance, Razorpay in India can be compared to Stripe in the U.S. to understand where payment platforms typically achieve profitability.

5. Intuitively Identify High-Margin Sub-Segments

Focus on areas with fewer competitors, lower costs, or higher willingness to pay. Ask, "Which parts of the customer experience would people pay a premium for?" Speak with customers or industry insiders to pinpoint areas of the value chain where they feel overcharged or underserved.

6. Look for Adjacent Opportunities

Adjacent markets or services can often be more profitable than the core business. Consider complementary products or services your customers might need. For example, Ola expanded its profit pools by entering premium services with Ola Prime.

7. Accept Directional Accuracy over Precision

Remember, profit pool analysis isn't about pinpoint accuracy but rather identifying broad, profitable trends. If necessary, focus on whether a segment is "high," "medium," or "low" profitability rather than attempting to calculate exact percentages. Knowing that premium skincare offers higher margins than mass-market products is sufficient to guide a D2C brand like Mamaearth.

Profit Pool Analysis in Action: Key Takeaways for Startups

1. **High-Volume, Low-Margin Is Not Sustainable**: Just because a segment generates high revenue doesn't mean it's a good place to invest. High-volume, low-margin segments may offer short-term returns but lack sustainability.

2. **Look for Small Niche Segments**: Smaller, niche segments can be surprisingly

profitable. These areas are often overlooked by larger competitors who focus on high-revenue opportunities because small scale is not attractive to them.

3. **Focus on Emerging Profit Pools**: Profit pools can shift as industries evolve, though generally over a long period of time. Staying aware of market trends, technological innovations, and consumer shifts is essential to capturing the most lucrative opportunities.

Foundational Tool 2: Revenue Models

The customer buys (or utilizes for free) a product from the company; how the company makes money from the customer (and the transactions) defines its revenue model. The revenue model answers the essential question: **How will you make money?** While profit pool analysis indicates where the most profitable areas lie, your revenue model serves as the blueprint that guides how you'll tap into those areas to generate revenue and profits.

From the perspective of startups, the business models they typically choose fall into one of the following categories based on their market, customer needs, and industry:

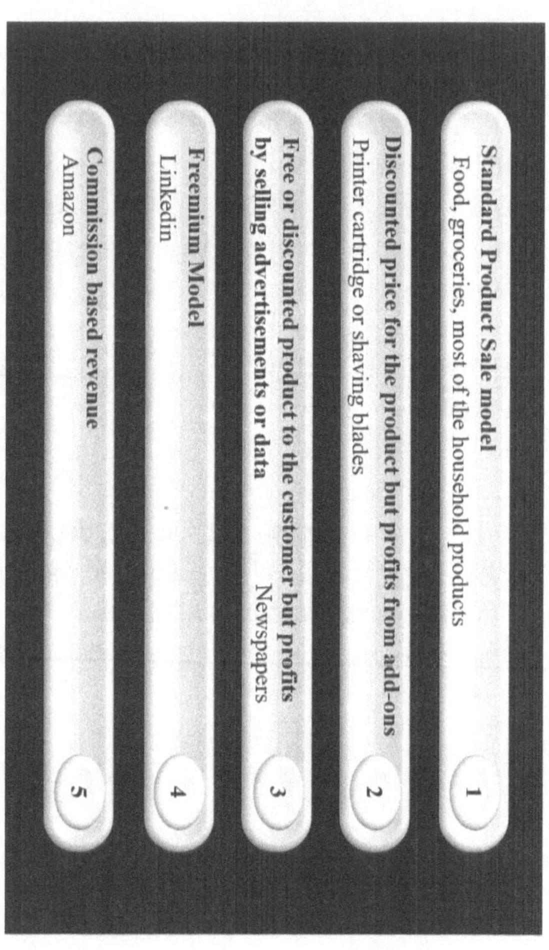

1. Standard Product Sale Model and Its Two Variants – D2C and Subscription-Based

The standard product sale model is the simplest and most traditional way of doing business—selling a product to customers in exchange for payment. This model is prevalent in industries like retail, consumer goods, and manufacturing, where the transaction involves a one-time exchange of goods for money. For example, Apple sells iPhones to consumers through its stores or online platforms, following the standard sale model.

Over time, startups have innovated on this basic model to include Direct-to-Consumer (D2C) and subscription-based sales, both of which allow businesses to address specific customer needs and optimize revenue generation.

Subscription Model: In the subscription business model, customers pay a recurring fee to access a product or service, creating a steady revenue stream for the company. This model works well for businesses offering digital services or products that provide ongoing value. For instance, Netflix generates stable and recurring revenue through monthly subscriptions, offering on-demand entertainment. The subscription model ensures predictable revenue, fosters customer loyalty, and enables rapid scaling once a solid customer base is established. Companies can focus on retention rather than constantly acquiring new customers, leading to better lifetime value (LTV).

D2C Model: The Direct-to-Consumer (D2C) business model allows companies to sell products directly to customers without relying on intermediaries. This model is common in industries like food, apparel, and health &

wellness. Warby Parker sells eyeglasses directly to consumers online, bypassing traditional retail distribution channels (though it now has exclusive stores to complement online sales). In India, Mamaearth initially sold its personal care products only directly through its website and online platforms like Amazon and Flipkart before utilizing offline channels.

D2C enables businesses to control the entire customer experience, save distribution costs by being online-only in the beginning, and capture a larger share of the profit pool by eliminating intermediaries. It also allows companies to collect customer data directly, improving personalization and retention strategies.

2. Discounted Price Model for the Product but Profits from Add-Ons

This model involves selling the core product at a low price (sometimes at cost or even below cost) while generating profits from add-ons, upgrades, or services associated with the product. Gaming consoles like PlayStation or Xbox are sold at a discounted price, but the companies earn significant revenue from game sales, online subscriptions, and accessories. In the printer industry, companies like HP sell printers at affordable prices but generate most of their profits from selling ink cartridges.

This model lowers the initial entry barrier for customers, enabling high adoption rates. Add-ons, often sold at higher margins, create a profitable ecosystem. Businesses can also achieve predictive revenue by ensuring customers stick to their products for ongoing needs.

3. **Revenue from Data/ Advertisement**

This model leverages customer data to generate revenue, often through targeted advertising or partnerships. It is commonly found in digital platforms, social media, and free-to-use apps. Google provides free services like Gmail, Google Search, and Maps but generates significant revenue by selling advertising space based on user behavior and search data. Facebook (now Meta) earns billions by utilizing its vast user data to offer highly targeted advertising solutions for businesses.

Platforms with massive user bases generate rich data, which becomes a lucrative asset. Advertisers value precise targeting, and businesses benefit from economies of scale as their user base grows. This model is particularly effective when paired with free or low-cost services that attract large audiences.

Many newspapers are priced very low to increase readership; the large readership is then offered to advertisers. If you examine the financials of newspapers, approximately 80% of their revenue comes from advertisements.

4. Freemium Model

The freemium business model offers basic services for free while charging for premium features, products, or services. It is widely used in SaaS, gaming, and digital platforms. Dropbox provides free storage up to a certain limit, while premium users pay for higher-capacity storage and additional features. In India, OTT platforms like Hotstar (Disney+) allow free streaming of some content but charge for premium content, live sports, or ad-free experiences. The low barrier to entry enables businesses to grow a large user base quickly. Once users experience the free product and find value in it, a subset transitions to premium offerings, generating sustainable revenue. This model also fosters loyalty, as customers are already familiar with the platform before upgrading.

5. Commission-Based Revenue (Platforms or Marketplaces)

A marketplace business model connects buyers and sellers, earning revenue by charging a commission for each transaction. This model is particularly prevalent in e-commerce, real estate, and service industries. Amazon and Flipkart act as intermediaries, connecting buyers and sellers while taking a commission on each sale. Urban Company in India connects customers with service providers (like electricians, cleaners, and beauty professionals) and charges a percentage of the service fee.

This model reduces the startup's need to carry inventory or directly manage operations, lowering risk and enabling scalability. As more buyers and sellers join the platform, the network effect strengthens, leading to exponential growth. This approach also ensures a diverse offering without requiring a company to specialize in every category. Importantly, the platform generates its commission even if the seller incurs a loss on the sale.

Considerations in choosing the Right Revenue Model for Your Startup:

- **Assess the Nature of Your Product**: Subscription works for services with recurring value e.g., Netflix or SaaS platforms, whereas standard sale model suits tangible products (e.g., D2C brands like Mamaearth). Freemium is ideal for digital products where a small subset pays for premium features (e.g., Dropbox). Clearly, add-on profits align with ecosystems where customers need accessories or ongoing services e.g., gaming consoles and games. Commission-Based models thrive in marketplaces (e.g. Urban Company).

- **Evaluate Competitive Landscape**: In crowded markets, use revenue models to create differentiation. E.g. in food delivery, Swiggy used a subscription plan (Swiggy One) for free delivery, creating a loyal customer base in a highly competitive space.

- **Think Scalability**: Subscription and Freemium models are typically more scalable, generating predictable, recurring revenues whereas D2C and Standard Sale models require effective scaling of production and logistics. Commission-based models scale quickly with the network effect (more users attract more providers and vice versa).

- **Consider Your Startup's Strengths**: If you have direct access to customers, D2C allows you to maximize profit margins. If you lack inventory or direct operations, commission-based models are ideal.

- **Evaluate Customer Behavior to see if there are preferences:** Would they pay for add-ons or premium features (Freemium or Add-Ons)? Or are they willing to share data or interact with advertisements for a free product (Data/Ads)?

- **Think About Monetization Timing:** Freemium and data/advertising models delay revenue generation in exchange for fast user acquisition. Subscription and D2C models prioritize monetization from the beginning.

Using Revenue Models for Differentiation

Access to data in D2C and subscription models cannot be replicated in traditional sale methods. Use that data to create experiences and tailor-made solutions and rewards. Leverage exclusivity - Spotify creates playlists tailored to individual listening habits, reinforcing customer loyalty. Two other possibilities are:

- Innovate Around Freemium: Offer value upfront for free while making premium features irresistible. Canva differentiated itself by offering easy-to-use graphic design tools for free, converting casual users into paying customers with premium templates and collaboration tools.
- Target Ecosystem Benefits: Add-On models thrive when the ecosystem adds value. Apple uses its ecosystem (MacBooks, iPhones, Apple Watches) to sell high-margin accessories and services like iCloud.

One could also combine models to create hybrid models. Hybrid models often work best, especially when targeting diverse revenue streams. Amazon combines standard product sales (own-brand items), commission-based marketplace (third-party sellers), and subscription (Prime).

Foundational Tool 3: Competitor Analysis

Competitor analysis is the process of identifying and evaluating the strengths, weaknesses, strategies, financials, product roadmaps, and market positions etc. of companies operating in the same industry or offering similar products or services. The objective is to find or confirm opportunities to carve out your own space in the market.

In the context of this book, competitor analysis plays a dual role. It's critical for shaping your working model, but it also weaves through the VIBE Framework. Whether you are validating your idea, identifying market size, building differentiation, or establishing strong economics, a robust understanding of the competitive landscape will help in every step.

Why Competitor Analysis is Essential for Startups:

1. Spot Gaps for Differentiation: Competitor analysis ensures you don't end up being a copy of existing players. Instead, it helps you identify opportunities to stand out.

2. Support for Strategic Decisions: Whether it's pricing, product features, or go-to-market strategies, competitor analysis ensures your decisions are grounded in market realities. By studying competitors,

you save time by learning what already works and what doesn't.

3. Mitigate Risks: A thorough understanding of competitors can help you anticipate threats, like pricing wars.

Framework for Competitor Analysis

The most versatile framework for competitor analysis is the **SWOT Analysis**, which evaluates:

Strengths: Identify what competitors excel at - trusted brands, economies of scale, strong distribution channels. From the point of view of D2C soap brand, the biggest strength of HUL or Marico lies in their extensive offline distribution network. It will be futile for a startup to compete with them in this domain.

Weaknesses: Spot gaps in their offerings e.g. poor customer service, limited geographic reach, lack of innovation. Uber initially struggled with local nuances in India, like auto-rickshaw integration, which Ola capitalized on.

Opportunities: Recognize emerging trends or underserved segments that competitors haven't yet addressed. In fact many times, the competitors recognize the opportunity but they cannot capitalize on it because of historical brand positioning or legacy processes or shareholder issues

Threats: Anticipate external challenges to your idea. There are two key issues a founder

needs to form a view on. The first is the expected response of the incumbents (or even other startups) in the form of aggressive pricing, new product launches etc. The second is the regulatory aspects- many startups are ahead of regulation that is they operate in areas where regulation has not yet caught up. E.g. when UBER launched in several countries, these countries had no regulation regarding ride sharing; the concept did not exist till the time UBER launched its service.

Tools and Methods for Competitor Analysis

- Primary Research - Customer Interviews and Surveys: Speak directly with competitors' customers to identify pain points. Use tools like Google Forms to gather insights on unmet needs in existing solutions.

- Secondary Research
    - o Industry Reports: Sources like PwC, KPMG, or government publications provide insights into market trends.
    - o Digital Tools: One can use *SEMrush* to analyze competitors' online presence, including traffic, keywords, and ad strategies. *Glassdoor* can help you understand internal challenges faced by competitors such as employee dissatisfaction or high attrition rates.

- o Public Data: For public companies, financial reports reveal revenue streams, cost structures, and growth areas. Reviewing Zomato's financial disclosures can highlight key data related to food delivery, dining-out services and quick commerce
- Real-Time Insights
  - o Monitor Social Media and Reviews: Platforms like Twitter, Facebook, and Google Reviews often highlight customer sentiments in real time. Social media feedback on Blinkit's delivery delays helped its competitors refine their operational models.
  - o Track Funding News: Platforms like YourStory or Crunchbase can provide alerts on funding or strategic pivots by competitors.

Using Competitor Analysis to Build the Working Model:

Competitor analysis directly supports the working model by helping founders make informed decisions:

1. Validate the Problem Statement: Identify whether competitors address the same pain points your startup aims to solve. If they do, how well are they solving it?

2. Refine the Solution: Look for gaps in competitors' offerings and adjust your solution to fill those voids. Ola introduced features like ride subscriptions and in-app safety alerts after analyzing Uber's shortcomings.

3. Determine Pricing: Use competitor pricing as a benchmark to position your offering. Mamaearth priced its premium personal care products competitively by studying both local (Himalaya) and global (The Body Shop) competitors.

4. Prioritize Market Segments: Competitor analysis helps identify underserved customer segments. Razorpay targeted small and medium businesses in the payments space, while Paytm focused on individuals initially.

5. Strengthen Differentiation: Use competitor weaknesses to build your unique selling proposition (USP). CRED differentiated itself from Paytm and PhonePe by focusing on premium users and rewards for timely credit card payments.

6. Anticipate Competitive Threats: Stay ahead of the curve by monitoring competitor moves and adjusting strategies accordingly.

Part 3: The VIBE Framework

Introduction: Part 3

With your working model established, it's time to transition from theoretical constructs to practical validation. Part 3 introduces The VIBE Framework, designed to rigorously assess and refine your startup idea across four critical dimensions:

1. **Validation**: Utilizing secondary resources plus engaging directly with potential customers and industry experts to confirm the demand for your solution

2. **Identifying Market Size**: Employing research to accurately estimate the scope and scale of your target market

3. **Building Differentiation**: Analyzing competitor offerings and market trends to clearly set your product apart

4. **Establishing Economics**: Ensure your business is economically viable by undertaking basic financial analysis

At this stage, you will build on the initial research and insights gathered so far. While the earlier stages relied on secondary data and your own expertise, The VIBE Framework may also require more direct inputs, such as:

- Talking to Experts: To validate assumptions and identify blind spots.

- Engaging with Potential Customers: To understand their needs and preferences.
- Studying Competitors: To refine positioning and uncover opportunities.

This framework allows you to thoroughly evaluate your idea from multiple angles, helping you refine it into a well-rounded, market-ready concept. However, it's also possible that your evaluation may reveal gaps that require a pivot or, in some cases, a decision to abandon the idea. This isn't failure—it is an outcome of a process to ensure time, resources, and energy are directed only toward ideas with the highest potential.

It is also important to point out that The VIBE Framework is not a linear process. It thrives as an iterative model, designed to evolve alongside your startup idea. Iteration is critical because no startup idea emerges fully formed, and the entrepreneurial journey involves refining assumptions, testing hypotheses, and aligning resources to create something viable and impactful.

Why Iteration Is Key?

The iterative nature of VIBE ensures flexibility. As a founder, you'll often discover that after completing one phase, such as Validation, you may need to revisit another phase—perhaps due to unforeseen challenges or insights. For instance:

- You validate your idea with potential customers, but their feedback suggests that a critical feature needs rethinking.
- Poor unit economics might prompt revisiting product differentiation so that higher price is acceptable to the customers

This flexibility prevents the stagnation of your idea, ensuring continual improvement until you arrive at the most compelling and feasible version.

How to Use VIBE Iteratively

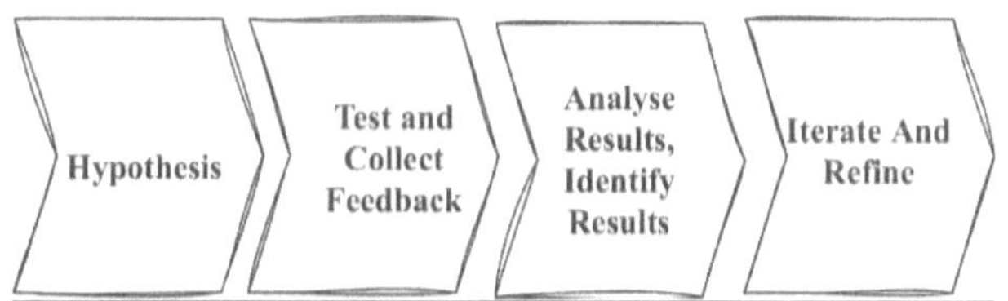

The iterative process of VIBE involves recognizing the interconnectedness of each step and actively seeking feedback loops. Here's a practical guide:

1. Start with Hypotheses: Begin each step with clear, testable hypotheses. For example:

- Validation: "Customers will pay for a subscription model for curated books."

- Market Sizing: "The TAM for book subscriptions is at least 2 million in the target segment."
- Differentiation: "Our AI-based recommendation engine is a unique moat."
- Economics: "LTV of a regular customer is 4 units or Rs. 2000 minimum"

2. Test and Collect Feedback: Use tools and methods suitable (and feasible) for each step:

- Validation: Surveys, interviews, landing pages, even prototype testing in some cases
- Market Sizing: Industry reports, government data, and competitor analysis
- Differentiation: Competitor mapping, user feedback, focus groups, feedback from experts
- Economics: Financial modeling, CAC/LTV calculations, sensitivity analysis, competitor data

3. Analyze Results and Identify Gaps: Evaluate the outcomes of your test; are there red flags? For example:

- Validation reveals weak demand for the primary feature
- TAM analysis shows insufficient market size to get investor interest

- Differentiation overlaps with competitors implying no real differentiation
- CAC is too high relative to LTV implying poor unit economics

4. Iterate and Refine: Based on identified gaps, revisit earlier steps:
- Adjust the product or service offering
- Reassess customer segments for market size
- Enhance differentiation through new USPs
- Modify the revenue model to improve financial viability

Keeping detailed records of each iteration is important. This not only helps in refining the idea but also creates a clear narrative for investors, showing how the idea evolved and improved through rigorous testing. If multiple iterations still show significant gaps, it may be time to pivot or reassess the viability of the idea altogether.

By the end of this part, if your idea passes through the VIBE Framework, you'll have a robust, validated concept ready for execution. Let's begin.

Chapter 4: Validating the Idea - Testing Before the Leap

As a founder, you've already made significant progress. You've used your experience, exposure, and understanding to develop an idea, and you've refined it into a working model using structured frameworks and research. Now comes the critical moment—putting your idea to the test.

The objective is simple yet crucial: get a clear, actionable understanding of the feasibility of your idea and its readiness to be turned into a business. While you've been weighing feasibility throughout this process till now also, Validation is where you make it definitive.

At this stage in the VIBE Framework, you'll focus on answering key questions:

- Does a real demand exist for your product or service?

- Are customers willing to pay for your solution?

- Are there any deal-breaking challenges you've overlooked?

This stage, **Validation**, is where your idea faces its most rigorous scrutiny yet. It's not about stress-testing in the traditional sense; it's about exposing your idea to independent, external inputs that challenge your assumptions, uncover hidden weaknesses, and confirm its potential. At this stage, you will undertake:

• Secondary Research: Deep dives further into market data, industry trends, and comparable case studies to confirm your hypotheses.

• Primary Research: Directly interacting with potential customers, industry experts, and even competitors to gather first-hand insights.

Secondary research "forms hypotheses", while primary research "confirms or disproves" them. Both are critical to understand the full picture. Validation doesn't guarantee success - it's impossible to eliminate all risks - but it minimizes uncertainty and gives you confidence in the direction you have taken.

In India, where markets are highly price-sensitive and diverse, validation takes on an even more critical role. The assumptions you start with might be significantly challenged when faced with regional, cultural, or socio-economic nuances.

The following steps can be followed to validate your startup idea:

Step 1: Traffic analysis (Google search volume, social media interest)

Step 2: Trend analysis (growth rate of similar products or market trends)

Step 3: Specially looking at US and China markets

Step 4: Audience feedback (surveys, feedback from potential customers)

Step 5: Engagement (e.g. testing through landing pages)

The first three steps are desk research whereas the last two are direct feedback from your potential customers.

Step 1: Traffic analysis

Traffic analysis involves studying online behavior and search trends to understand demand. It's a cost-effective starting point that provides early indicators of market interest.

How to Conduct Traffic Analysis:

- Use Google Trends: Enter relevant keywords and observe their popularity over time and geography. For example, if your startup idea involves vegan snacks, search for terms like "vegan snacks," "healthy eating," or "plant-based diets."
- SEO Tools: Tools like SEMrush or Ubersuggest can show the search volume for specific keywords and related terms. This indicates how many people are searching for products or solutions in your domain.
- Competitor Analysis: Examine the online and media presence of competitors. Are they investing heavily in ads? What keywords do they rank for?

Example: A founder exploring a subscription box for sustainable fashion might notice consistent search interest for "sustainable clothing brands" but minimal ads for "sustainable clothing". In further analysis, it can be observed that no brand is focusing on it. This gap could be an opportunity.

Step 2: Trend analysis

When validating a startup idea, understanding trends is one of the most critical components. Trends provide context, highlight opportunities, and expose risks, offering a deeper understanding of whether the idea is aligned with market shifts and customer preferences. Trend mapping encompasses analyzing historical growth rates, studying competitors, observing socioeconomic changes, and learning from international markets. This process ensures that the idea is rooted in reality and poised to capitalize on evolving dynamics.

Beware of fads: A fad is a short-lived trend, craze, or phenomenon that gains rapid popularity but quickly fades away. Fads are often driven by novelty, media attention, or social influence rather than lasting value or practicality. Unlike trends, which may evolve and last for years, fads are typically fleeting. They rely on excitement, novelty, or the fear of missing out (FOMO). Fads have low practicality and lack long-term utility or substance. An example of a fad is a Fidget Spinner- a toy that gained massive popularity in 2017 before quickly declining. Businesses can leverage fads for short-term gains but must avoid overinvesting, as the appeal is unlikely to last. For startups, distinguishing between fads and long-term trends is critical to avoid chasing fleeting opportunities at the expense of building a sustainable business.

Mapping trends is about more than just understanding what is happening; it's about predicting where things are headed as well. A well-executed trend analysis covers the following:

1. Growth Rates of Similar Products or Services: Analyzing the historical and projected growth rates of analogous products or industries is crucial. Growth rates provide a sense of how much demand exists and whether it is expanding or contracting. How to Analyze:

- Look for reports on industry trends (e.g. from firms like McKinsey, Statista, or IBISWorld).
- Study financial disclosures of public companies in the same space.
- Analyze historical sales data of similar products.

Key Patterns to Watch:
- Consistent upward trends over multiple years
- Spikes due to specific events (e.g., health scares or regulatory changes)
- Seasonal variations and their underlying reasons

2. Competitor Analysis: Understanding the competitive landscape helps in doing trend analysis for the idea. Competitor analysis involves identifying who is already in the space, what they offer, and how they position themselves. Steps to Conduct Competitor Analysis:

- Identify Direct and Indirect Competitors: Direct competitors offer similar products, while indirect competitors fulfill the same customer need differently
- Study Offerings: Understand the features, pricing, and customer base of competitors
- Evaluate Performance: Analyze customer reviews, financial performance (if available), and market share
- Spot Gaps: Identify underserved customer segments or unmet needs

A fintech startup exploring SME lending might analyze how incumbents like LendingKart or NeoGrowth target small businesses. The startup could spot an opportunity to offer niche products, like loans tailored for freelancers.

3. Socioeconomic and Demographic Shifts: Socioeconomic changes significantly influence market demand. Factors such as population growth, aging demographics, urbanization, and income distribution shifts and shapes consumer behavior and preferences.

Sources of Data can include Government census data, World Bank and IMF reports, local development surveys and industry publications.

A childcare startup might find that dual-income households are rising in urban India, driving demand for daycare solutions. Simultaneously, demographic data confirms the growth in the number of working women, reinforcing the need for childcare services.

Looking for intersections between multiple trends (e.g., rising urbanization and increased smartphone adoption) is important to forecast the need for your products.

How to Identify Patterns in Trends

Mapping trends is not just about collecting data; it's about interpreting it to identify meaningful patterns.

It is very important to look for correlations. Identifying how one trend affects another is key. For example, increased smartphone penetration correlates with a rise in mobile-first solutions. Secondly, deviations from the norm often indicate emerging opportunities. For instance, a sudden surge in fitness app downloads could signify a lasting shift toward home workouts. One could use visualization Tools such as like charts, heat maps, and infographics can make patterns more apparent.

Some common pitfalls in Trend mapping that need to be avoided are as following:

- Overreliance on Historical Data: Past trends don't always predict future behavior. For example, demand for certain products may plateau as markets mature.
- Ignoring Contradictory Data: Confirmation bias can lead to dismissing data that doesn't align with preconceived ideas.

Step 3: Specifically Look At U.S. and China

When validating your startup idea, looking beyond your local market and analyzing trends from the U.S. and Chinese markets can provide invaluable cues. These two economies are often at the forefront of innovation and consumer behavior evolution. While your local market may differ in income levels, culture, and infrastructure, the trajectory of these global leaders often offers a glimpse into the future of your sector.

Why Study the U.S. and China?

- Innovation Hubs: Both markets are home to pioneering companies and technologies. The U.S. gave the world Amazon, Uber, and Airbnb, while China introduced giants like Alibaba, Meituan, and TikTok. Studying these innovations can inspire ideas on how to adapt similar models to the local ecosystem.

- Consumer Evolution: Over the past two decades, these markets have undergone rapid shifts in consumer behavior, driven by rising disposable incomes, digital adoption, and urbanization. The U.S. evolved from brick-and-mortar retail to e-commerce dominance. China leapfrogged traditional credit card use, going directly to mobile payments like Alipay and WeChat Pay.
- Scalability Insights: Startups in both markets are masters at scaling operations, especially in sectors like e-commerce, social commerce, and mobility. Understanding how they optimized logistics, reduced costs, and built trust with customers can provide key insights for your scaling journey.

Consumer-facing startups need to be aware of the following pitfalls when getting inferences rom the USA and China markets:

- Adjust for Market Differences: Income levels, purchasing power, and consumer priorities differ. For instance, premium products like Peloton thrive in the U.S., while in developing markets, affordability-focused models like Cult.Fit (fitness subscriptions) gain traction.
- Adopt, Don't Copy: It's tempting to replicate successful models, but direct copying rarely works. Instead, adapt ideas to local nuances. For instance the U.S. ride-hailing model

inspired Ola in India, but Ola differentiated itself by including auto-rickshaws and cash payments, a uniquely Indian need.

- Observe and experiment with sector-specific cues: China's "live-stream shopping" format, popularized by platforms like Taobao, has started influencing markets globally. If you're in retail, consider testing live selling formats locally.
- Use global trends as hypotheses but validate them locally through surveys, interviews, or pilot launches.

Examples of Lessons from the U.S. and China:

- India's E-commerce Growth: Flipkart studied Amazon's customer-centric model in the U.S. and adapted it by offering cash-on-delivery, addressing India's low credit card penetration.
- Paytm Mall was inspired by Alibaba's ecosystem model, leveraging both digital and offline channels.
- Byju's gamified learning experience took cues from U.S. platforms like Khan Academy but localized it for Indian students with multilingual options and exam-specific content.

- China's VIPKid demonstrated how one-on-one online tutoring could work globally, which inspired Indian startups like Vedantu.

Step 4: Audience Feedback

Audience engagement validates your idea by interacting with potential customers online or offline. The goal is to gauge their interest, understand their pain points, and refine your offering.

How to Engage with Your Audience:

- Social Media Polls and Posts: Platforms like Instagram, LinkedIn, or Twitter are excellent for gauging reactions. For example, you could post: "Would you subscribe to a service delivering personalized sustainable clothing monthly?"
- Forums and Communities: Engage with niche groups on Reddit, Discord, or Facebook. If your idea targets pet owners, visit forums dedicated to pets and ask questions or share your concept.
- Email Campaigns: Use tools like Mailchimp to run a small email campaign. Share your idea and track how many people click to learn more. A founder considering a fitness app for postpartum mothers might join parenting forums and discover specific pain points, like finding time for short, effective workouts.

- Social Proof - Surveys and Interviews: Surveys and interviews are more structured ways to understand customer needs, preferences, and willingness to pay. While conducting surveys, keep them short, focused and limit number of questions to 5-7. Ask Specific Questions for example Instead of "Do you like this idea?" ask, "How much would you pay for a service that delivers personalized eco-friendly meals weekly?" Incentivize responses by offering a discount or free resource for completing the survey.

  Similarly while conducting interviews let customers share their thoughts freely. Avoid asking leading questions e.g. instead of asking, "Don't you think this product is great?" ask, "What challenges do you face with existing solutions?"

  A founder building a pet grooming service might discover through interviews that convenience outweighs cost for many customers, leading them to offer home-based grooming appointments.

Step 5: Early Engagement

Early engagement can be triggered by:

- Landing Pages: Create a simple website that explains your product and includes a call-to-action, like signing up for early access.

- Pre-Orders: Offer a pre-sale of your product to gauge demand before production.
- Wizard of Oz MVP: Simulate your product manually before automating it. For example, instead of creating an app for meal deliveries, coordinate deliveries yourself to test demand.

Dropbox famously validated its idea by releasing a video that demonstrated its functionality, even before building the actual product. Evaluating Results of early engagement objectively is very important; validation is incomplete without analyzing and interpreting the data. The key is to identify patterns and insights that either confirm or challenge your assumptions.

Guidelines to Evaluate Results are following:
- Quantify Responses: What percentage of survey participants said they would pay for your product?
- Track Engagement: If 1,000 people visited your landing page, how many signed up or clicked "Buy Now"?
- Identify Red Flags: Low engagement or negative feedback isn't necessarily a failure. It's an opportunity to pivot or refine your idea.

Example: If only 5% of visitors to a sustainable skincare landing page signed up, it might indicate unclear messaging or a lack of demand. The founder could revisit their value proposition or target a different demographic.

While validation is critical, it's not foolproof. Here are some common mistakes at this stage:

- Confirmation Bias: Only seeking data that supports your idea. Actively look for opposing viewpoints.
- Ignoring Negative Feedback: If customers point out flaws, take them seriously and iterate.
- Over-Reliance on Desk Research: Market reports can indicate trends, but they don't replace direct customer input.

At the end of validation, you should have a clear understanding of whether your idea has demand. Insights into customer preferences and pain points would have been generated. Initial data to present to investors, including engagement metrics and pre-sales should now be available.

The Power & Significance of Zeitgeist in Idea Validation

In the fast-paced world of startups, one of the most crucial factors that determine success or failure is whether your idea resonates with the "zeitgeist"—the spirit of the times. Zeitgeist refers to the prevailing cultural, economic, and social climate that influences the attitudes and behaviors of people during a particular period. In other words, it's about being in tune with the world around you and spotting trends and movements before they fully unfold. As a founder, understanding zeitgeist is critical for validating whether your idea is genuinely aligned with where the world is heading—or whether you're simply chasing an outdated concept.

When you understand the zeitgeist, you are tapping into the collective energy and needs of society. You're offering something that fits into a larger narrative, something that aligns with the evolving mindset of your potential customers. It's the difference between launching a business idea that fades into obscurity and one that becomes a cultural movement.

As a startup, timing is everything. A good idea launched too early or too late can fail. If you launch before the market is ready, you risk having too few customers, and if you launch too late, competitors may have already captured the market. Understanding the zeitgeist helps you gauge when the world is ready for your idea. It's about identifying emerging shifts in consumer behavior, technology, or culture that signal the right time to act.

For instance, when Uber first launched, the concept of ride-sharing wasn't entirely new, but Uber was perfectly positioned to capture the zeitgeist of urban millennials seeking convenience, affordability, and flexibility in transportation.

More importantly, Zeitgeist provides the context to evaluate your idea's relevance. When you assess whether your idea fits into the current cultural, economic, and technological landscape, you're essentially finding if there a genuine demand for what you are offering.

For example, TikTok was born at the intersection of the growing demand for short-form, highly engaging video content and the rise of mobile-first generation. TikTok perfectly captured the zeitgeist of the moment by creating a platform where users could express themselves creatively, instantaneously, and often humorously. TikTok wasn't simply a copy of Vine or Instagram.

Understanding the Zeitgeist also helps in spotting emerging trends in case you are looking for ideas. The shifts might be in technology, social behavior, consumer values, or even politics. When you catch the right wave early on, you have the chance to build something that resonates deeply with the masses.

So, before you dive into product development or scaling, ask yourself: Does your startup tap into the zeitgeist? Are you responding to the underlying currents of change, or are you missing the pulse of what people really want? The more in sync you are with the moment, the higher your chances of building something truly impactful.

Chapter 5: Identifying Market Size

In this chapter, we will explore the crucial process of evaluating the potential market size for your startup idea. Market sizing forms the foundation of an idea evaluation, developing a robust business plan, offering insights into the scale of opportunity and shaping strategies for product development, marketing, and funding. Whether you're pitching to investors or building an internal roadmap, understanding market size is vital.

Why is Market Sizing Important?

Market sizing "partly' answers the fundamental question – does it make sense at all to pursue this idea? Only partly answers because the detailed economic analysis will add to the final answer - but to start with the size of the market is important to answer the fundamental question: Is it worth pursuing?

Generally speaking one would want a large market:

1. A large market means there is a broader base of potential customers, providing startups the opportunity to grow their revenue over time - there is room for growth.
2. Even if the startup captures only a small portion of the market, the potential for

significant revenue is higher compared to a smaller market.

3. Large markets provide more opportunities for eventual liquidity. Companies operating in large markets are often valued higher by acquirers or public market investors because they promise more revenue and growth opportunities in the future.

In addition estimation of the market size provides strategic clarity as founders can make informed decisions about resource allocation, product focus, and growth trajectories.

__Profitability in Niche Markets:__ Not every startup needs a massive market to succeed. While large, scalable markets often attract the most attention from venture capitalists due to their potential for exponential growth, smaller niche markets offer unique opportunities for startups with a focused approach. In these markets, startups can often achieve profitability faster and with fewer resources, as competition tends to be lower, and the customer base is more defined.

Operating in a niche market often comes down to the personal aspirations of the founders. Some founders are driven by the desire to create a sustainable, profitable business rather than chasing unicorn-level growth. These entrepreneurs may prioritize personal satisfaction, a steady income, or making a meaningful impact in a specific industry or community over achieving massive scale.

Nurturing Green, an Indian startup, operates in the niche market of gifting plants. Instead of competing in the crowded gift market dominated by flowers, chocolates, and personalized items, the company carved out a unique niche by offering eco-friendly, live plants as gifts.

Why It Works:

I.   Focused Audience: Their target customers include environmentally conscious individuals and corporates looking for unique gifting options.

II.   Differentiated Offering: Plants not only make for memorable gifts but also align with sustainability trends, making them more meaningful than traditional gifts.

III.   Loyal Customer Base: Companies and individuals who value sustainability are more likely to return for repeat purchases or refer others.

While Nurturing Green may not appeal to venture capitalists seeking rapid scalability, it demonstrates how focusing on a niche can build a profitable and sustainable business.

If your idea builds on an existing product, market sizing becomes relatively straightforward, using historical data and trends. However, for completely novel ideas, it requires creative approaches and robust research.

Irrespective, TAM-SAM-SOM is the most common framework used by the startup eco-system.

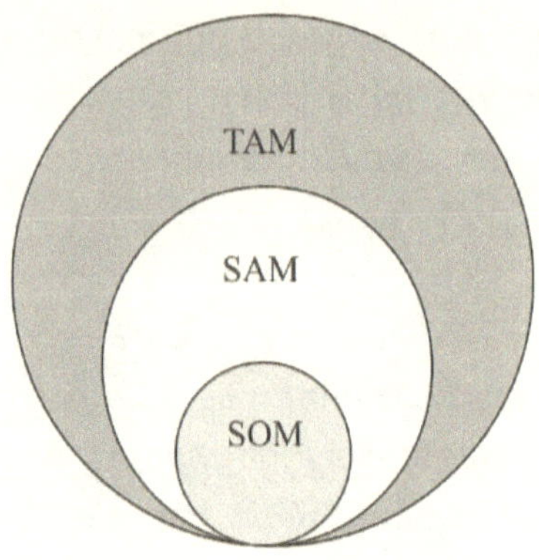

1. Total Addressable Market (TAM)

TAM represents the total demand for your product or service if you could capture the entire market. While it's aspirational, TAM helps gauge the ultimate potential of your idea.

Methods to calculate TAM

    I.   Top-Down Approach: Leverage macro-level data, such as industry reports and government publications, to estimate the market size. For instance, if you're launching an online education platform, research the global education market, which might be valued at $10 trillion, to set a broad benchmark.

II.	Bottom-Up Approach: Build TAM using individual customer data. For example, if you're selling a subscription-based fitness app at $120/year, and there are 50 million potential customers as per surrogate data (e.g. the number of people who buy protein shakes) globally, your TAM is $6 billion/year.

2. Serviceable Available Market (SAM)

SAM narrows down the TAM to the specific portion of the market your startup can realistically address. SAM is where the rubber meets the road. This involves accounting for your geographical reach, product scope, and operational capabilities. Founders often struggle to define SAM accurately, resulting in overestimations or ambiguous positioning.

SAM has to align with the startup's operational realities - Does the startup have the team, infrastructure, and partnerships to serve this market? Are the chosen customer segments reachable given the startup's resources that will be available to them? Do these customer segments have a really pressing pain point that can be solved by the startup?

Basically you have to identify your target segments here. Segmentation is the process of dividing your market into smaller groups to identify high-priority targets. Several possible ways to create a segmentation has been shown in the following diagram.

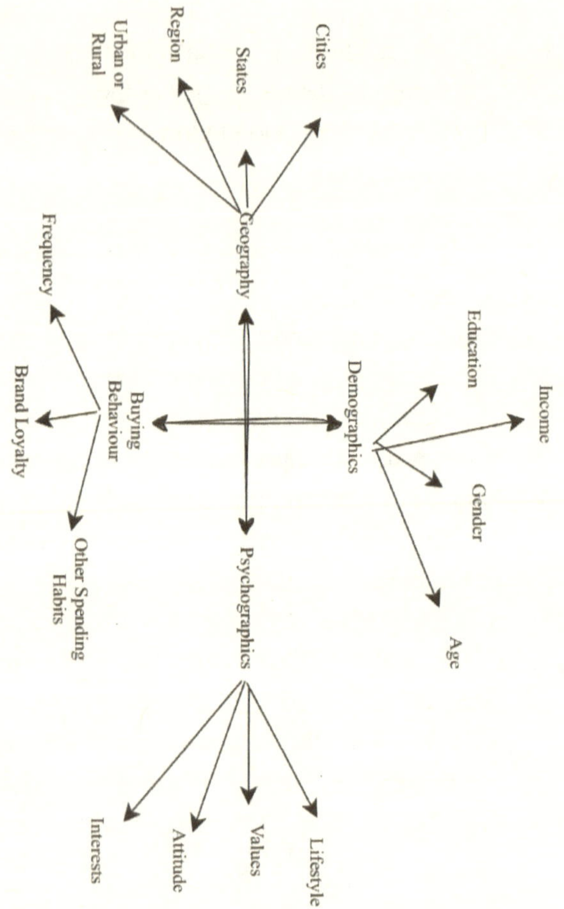

Factors Affecting SAM:

    i.   Distribution Channels: Are you equipped to distribute nationally or globally?

ii. Product Fit: Does your product resonate with specific demographics or geographies?

iii. Legal and Regulatory Constraints: Are there barriers to entry in certain regions?

3. Serviceable Obtainable Market (SOM)

SOM is the realistic market share you can achieve in the short to medium term, considering competition, resources, and scalability.

Key Considerations for SOM:

I. Competitive Landscape: Who are the dominant players, and how saturated is the market?

II. Go-to-Market Strategy: How effectively can you penetrate the market?

III. Financial Constraints: Do you have the resources to achieve significant market penetration? And looking from the other side, does this market share justify setting up the business? If the projected market share is too small (because of the segments targeted or lack of resources) then competition can easily challenge you. This part is iterative with the last part of the VIBE framework (Establish Economics) and you will have to achieve a balance with available resources, Unit economics, customer acquisition cost and achievable market share.

Accurate market sizing relies on robust data. Both Quantitative and Qualitative Analysis needs to be done – this implies combining numbers with insights to create a complete picture.

VCs are inundated with pitch decks showcasing massive Total Addressable Markets (TAM). Founders frequently highlight their multi-billion-dollar market opportunities, projecting that capturing even a small percentage could lead to substantial revenues.

While TAM, SAM (Serviceable Addressable Market), and SOM (Serviceable Obtainable Market) are crucial frameworks for understanding market potential, they can also be a double-edged sword. If misinterpreted or overstated, they may lead to flawed investment decisions. Many founders use top-down approaches to calculate TAM, often citing third-party reports or market research firms like Gartner or McKinsey. While these numbers lend credibility, they are frequently overgeneralized. Large TAM numbers often ignore market heterogeneity. For instance, while the global fitness industry might have a TAM of $100 billion, it includes gyms, equipment manufacturers, apps, personal trainers, and supplements. A single startup is unlikely to serve all segments effectively. Pay attention to regulatory, cultural, or technological barriers as well that might stymie growth.

SOM is the litmus test for execution. SOM is often overlooked or underestimated, yet it provides the clearest view of a startup's execution

plan. SOM isn't just about numbers - it's about how effectively a startup can penetrate its target market. Excessive optimism without data needs to be avoided. Macro trends, regulations, and cultural barriers have to be taken into account as one moves from TAM to SAM to SOM calculations. A fintech startup targeting rural India might have a large SAM but struggle with digital literacy and internet access.

Niche Dominance as a Strategy

Startups that succeed often start small and dominate a niche before expanding. Amazon began with books, Uber with black cars, and Airbnb with budget-conscious travelers. Instead of chasing a massive TAM, startups focus on a smaller SAM and prove their ability to execute within a smaller segment. A founder who can achieve 50% SOM in a $10 million market is often more investable than one chasing 1% of a $10 billion TAM.

Eventually you can expand your SAM once you have achieved success in your segments. TAM comes back into play as a long-term vision (rather than an immediate target) by the following strategies:

1. Product Innovation: Offering new features or services that cater to adjacent customer segments

2. Geographic Expansion: Scaling operations to new regions or countries
3. Customer Retention and Upselling: Increasing revenue from existing customers by adding complementary products
4. Identifying Market Adjacencies: Market adjacencies refer to related markets that your product can expand into in the future. Adjacencies can be identified in the following way:
    I. Analyze Customer Needs: What related problems can your product solve?
    II. Study Competitors: Explore additional services/products offered by competitors
    III. Monitor Trends: Look for emerging opportunities in adjacent spaces

Example: A company offering HR software for SMEs might identify adjacencies in payroll management, employee engagement, or training solutions.

Chapter 6: Building Differentiation

Differentiation is the key to standing out in a competitive landscape; differentiation lies at the heart of every successful startup. It defines what sets you apart from competitors, captures customer loyalty, and draws investors to back your vision. In a startup ecosystem brimming with ideas, the ability to stand out is often the difference between being wiped out and monumental success. Without differentiation, a business risks becoming indistinguishable, leaving little reason for customers or investors to choose it over others.

Startups inherently operate in uncertain and dynamic environments. With limited resources and time, they must demonstrate a unique value proposition to build momentum before competitors, especially larger incumbents or well-funded copycats, replicate their idea. Differentiation doesn't only provide a competitive edge; it buys the time and resources required to establish a firm foothold before the uniqueness is copied. Eventually everything is copy-able.

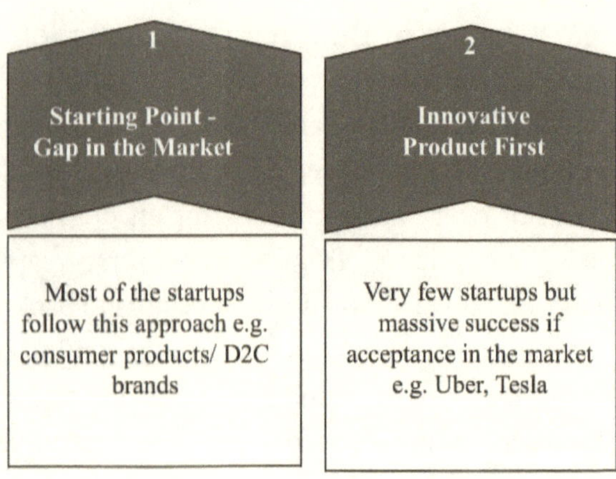

This image presents two key differentiation approaches adopted by startups to stand out in competitive markets:

1. **Product Design Addressing a Market Gap**:

    I. Startups in this category focus on identifying unmet needs in the market and designing products to fill those gaps.

    II. Direct-to-Consumer (D2C) brands are prominent examples, with most startups aligning with this approach.

2. **Innovative Product First, Seeking a Market**:

    I. This approach involves creating groundbreaking products and then creating a market for them.

II. While fewer startups take this path, those that do often achieve massive success if the product gains market acceptance. Examples include technology led transformative companies like Uber and Tesla.

This categorization highlights how startups choose either a market-driven strategy or a product-first innovation strategy to achieve differentiation and growth.

Why Differentiation Matters
Differentiation matters because customers and investors are overwhelmed by choices. For customers, it's about choosing a product or service that addresses their needs in a superior way. For investors, it's about identifying a business with sustainable growth potential and barriers that protect its market position.

Elaborating, differentiation is critical because of the following reasons:

1. Customer Attraction and Retention: Differentiated offerings resonate more deeply with specific audiences. A clear and unique value proposition drives loyalty and word-of-mouth growth.

2. Price Elasticity: Differentiation allows startups to charge a premium. Customers willingly

pay more for products that deliver perceived added value, whether through superior design, technology, or brand appeal.

3. Market Positioning: It defines your place in the market. A differentiated startup positions itself as a leader or innovator in its niche, often dominating its category.

4. Investor Confidence: Differentiation reduces risk. It signals that the startup has a defensible position, even in competitive markets.

Founders are biased to overstate the level of differentiation of their business due to a psychological, strategic, and contextual factors. Founders are typically deeply passionate about their ideas. This passion can lead to optimism bias, where they overestimate the uniqueness and potential of their product or service. They genuinely believe their offering is groundbreaking. There are other reasons for this bias:

Need to Impress Investors: During pitches, founders are under pressure to make their startup stand out. They may exaggerate differentiation to secure funding, presenting their idea as more defensible and innovative than it is in reality.

A fintech startup might claim its AI-powered fraud detection is "proprietary" and impossible to replicate, even though similar solutions exist in the market. The competitive nature of fundraising often incentivizes founders to embellish their differentiators to attract attention and outshine rivals.

Tunnel Vision and Lack of Perspective: Founders often operate in an echo chamber, surrounded by a team and stakeholders who are equally invested in shared success. This environment can create confirmation bias, where founders only see evidence supporting their belief in the product's uniqueness.

Overlooking the Replication Factor: Founders often underestimate how quickly competitors can replicate certain aspects of their product or service. They may overstate the defensibility of their differentiation.

A food-tech startup might claim its logistics algorithm is a strong moat, unaware that larger competitors with more resources can build similar or better algorithms. Differentiation that lacks significant replication barriers is unlikely to provide long-term competitive advantage.

Emotional Attachment to the Idea: Founders are emotionally invested in their startup, often seeing it as an extension of themselves. This emotional connection can lead to inflated claims about its uniqueness. A founder of an artisanal coffee brand may claim their blend is "unlike anything in the market" due to personal pride. The emotional bias of founders can skew their perception of differentiation.

Differentiation and the Idea Shaking Framework

In the Idea Shaker, differentiation is baked into certain categories of startup ideas by default. For example, ideas in the quadrant of "Tech as Core – New Product" naturally exhibit high differentiation because they bring innovations that disrupt the status quo. Consider startups like SpaceX or OpenAI, whose groundbreaking technology redefined their industries.

But differentiation isn't limited to tech. Startups in traditional sectors also require unique elements to thrive. For instance, Lenskart's Omni channel strategy or FirstCry's focus on baby products tapped into underserved markets while establishing strong moats against competition. Differentiation is essential across all idea categories, as no startup survives by being generic.

Moreover, differentiation offers something invaluable: runway. Startups need sufficient time to develop and scale their business before copycats or larger players swoop in. Whether through a proprietary algorithm, an exclusive partnership, or a unique brand, differentiation buys that time.

Examples of Successful Differentiation
- **India:**
  - Ola Cabs: Differentiated itself by offering local solutions tailored to the

Indian market, such as auto-rickshaw rides and localized payment options.

o Zomato: Initially set itself apart with comprehensive restaurant listings and then pivoted to food delivery, leveraging its brand familiarity.

- **USA:**

o Airbnb: Redefined travel by turning ordinary homes into accommodations. Its differentiation stemmed from a community-driven approach and unique inventory that hotels couldn't replicate.

o Tesla: Combined innovation in electric vehicles with luxury design and environmental appeal, creating a brand that stood apart from legacy automakers.

Differentiation can be achieved by using one or any combination of the following factors:

Unique product and service (along with the right positioning): At the heart of differentiation is offering something distinctive—whether it's a groundbreaking solution, an innovative product, or an enhanced version of an existing service. Zerodha disrupted the brokerage industry in India by introducing a low-cost trading platform, radically different from traditional brokers charging high commissions.

Technology Advantage: Proprietary technology or intellectual property (IP) often forms the backbone of differentiation. This could include unique algorithms, advanced manufacturing techniques, or AI-based personalization. Byju's leveraged its app's gamified and interactive learning experience to distinguish itself in the ed-tech space.

Access to Exclusive Resources: Differentiation can also come from access—be it to suppliers, partners, or distribution channels that others cannot easily replicate. Flipkart's early access to private equity funding allowed it to build a robust supply chain and logistics network, enabling faster delivery and a wider inventory.

Differentiation requires an iterative approach - and it is a continuous process to ensure that it doesn't get easily copied. This could involve building a strong brand, creating a loyal customer base, or patenting key technologies. Patagonia's focus on sustainability and its commitment to ethical production have built a brand moat that competitors find hard to replicate. Amazon initially differentiated with book selection and pricing. Over time, it added convenience (Prime), a vast product range, and even its own hardware (Kindle) to stay ahead.

Replication Barrier: The Most Defensible Layer on any Moat

The strongest form of differentiation typically depends on the industry and context, but Replication Barrier is most important indicator. Replication barriers make it inherently difficult for competitors to copy the product, service, or business model. These can stem from proprietary technology, regulatory advantages, trade secrets, or economies of scale that others can't easily achieve. While all types of differentiation will help a startup initially stand out, replication barriers ensure long-term competitive advantage. Even if competitors notice your success, they face significant hurdles trying to replicate or surpass your offering.

Google's algorithms and infrastructure are a significant replication barrier. Competitors have tried to build alternatives, but the scale, data, and continuous improvement Google has achieved remain unmatched. SpaceX's first-mover advantage in reusable rocket technology created a replication barrier, supported by years of research, development, and cost reductions.

Strong branding and identity can be powerful, but they are vulnerable if not paired with something unique. A competitor with better execution or marketing can erode a purely brand-led differentiation.

Technology as a differentiator is strong, but it's strongest when it cannot be replicated over time (protected by patents, trade secrets, or continuous innovation). Tesla's initial advantage in electric vehicles was technological, but competitors are rapidly catching up. Tesla relies on scaling, branding, and a network of superchargers now to maintain its edge.

However, industry context always matters - in tech-heavy industries, technology advantage and replication barriers are intertwined. Proprietary algorithms, patents, or scalable platforms can create significant differentiation. In consumer-focused industries, superior product or services plays a bigger role initially, but replication barriers (e.g., brand loyalty or network effects) ensure longevity whereas in B2B sectors, access to exclusive partnerships or superior distribution channels can be vital but needs to be coupled with something harder to replicate.

It's very important to understand that the strongest differentiation is often layered - the best startups combine multiple forms of differentiation. For example:

- Amazon: Combines replication barriers (logistics and infrastructure), strategic positioning (customer obsession), and access (vendor relationships).
- Zomato (India): Blends strategic positioning (local expertise), access (restaurant partnerships), and replication barriers (delivery logistics, app usability).

A strong replication barrier forms the foundation, but layering other forms of differentiation creates a more robust and sustainable advantage.

Chapter 7: Establishing Economics

Establishing Economics is the final analysis that a founder needs to do to his or her startup idea. This stage is the last because it takes into account all the business attributes finalized so far, and determines whether a profitable business can be created from the idea. If not, you may need to go back to the drawing board and make changes to the working model. The output of this stage (and of the VIBE framework) should be a "profitable - implementable business model".

The fundamental objective of doing financial analysis of any startup is to see whether it will eventually make profits or not.

The key question is - why are profits important for a startup?

Achieving profits is the ultimate goal of any business as it makes it an independent entity with no reliance on external sources of capital. If a business doesn't generate its own profits, it will be dependent on external capital to survive. In the startup world, high growth to capture market share almost always comes at the cost of delaying profits. Investors fund this requirement with the expectation that the delayed profits will be much higher than immediate ones. But a lot of times when the funding cycle turns (i.e. when the investors stop investing in startups in an economic downturn as they perceive startups are riskier than normal times) there is no more external capital available for investment. At that time the startup will get into distress and it may even shut down. So essentially the objective of any business is to move towards profit as soon as possible because that ensures that it can make its own decisions, raise debt, hire people, invest in growth etc.

Secondly, when the shares are listed on the stock market, the public market investors are evaluating against several investment options and they have low risk (and low patience) levels. They are not willing to take a risk on an investment which is still not profitable and has a risk of survival if the funding cycle changes. The share price of a listed mature startup reflects its profit making ability. Now obviously the valuation of any startup at early stages is a backward calculation from the eventual estimated share price when it is listed. Therefore evaluation of the startup at all stages (seed stage to Series A, to Series B, to Series C, etc.) is all driven by some kind of measurement of future profits. As a founder the only question that deserves your attention whenever you have to take a decision is how does it affect profits or future profits?

Many times you would have seen that business is making huge losses, sometimes in billions of dollars and still it's getting higher and higher valuation, and it's still able to attract funding. The only reason for that is its scale, probability and timeline of its profits have improved.

At an early stage of the startup, it's very difficult to estimate future profits as there is no data. Pseudo indicators come into play.

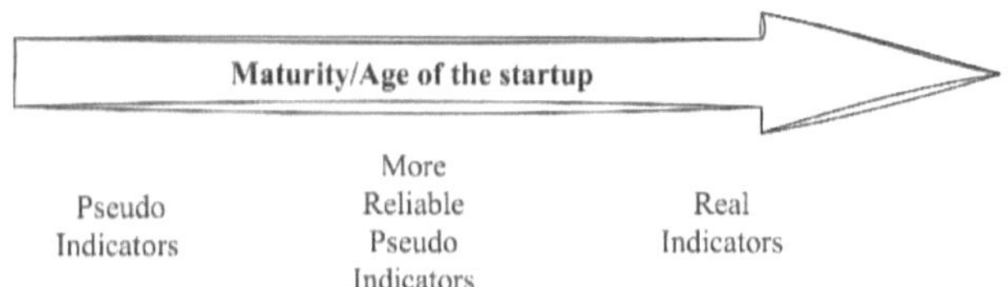

The analysis is subjective in the beginning, and moves more and more data based as the startup creates track record. Till that time, pseudo indicators are used to estimate profits.

This is where the "Unit Economics" become important. At an early stage, you cannot estimate market share, competitive reaction etc. but you have data related to a unit of transaction. Unit economics is financial analysis related to single transaction. Eventually, the entire business is created out of several "unit transactions" only, so the objective is to extract as much information as possible from unit economics so as to estimate future profits, its timeline and other attributes.

There are two key components of unit level economics:

1. LTV- CAC Analysis
2. The three contribution margins

The LTV- CAC metric

Let's start with the basic equation for calculating profits.

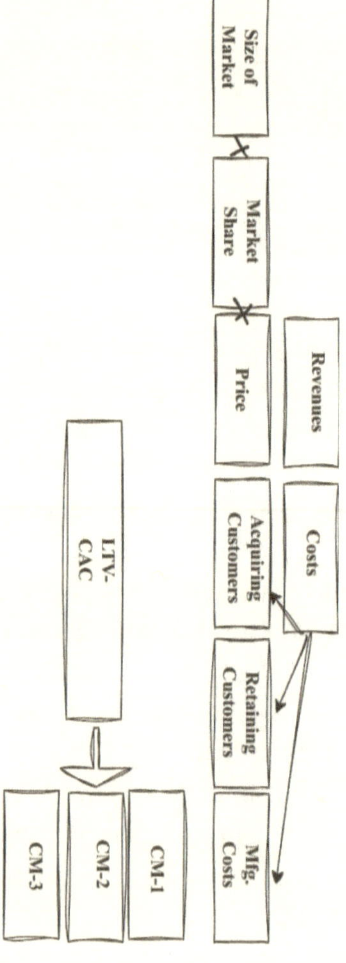

Profits are very simply the difference between the revenue on one side and the cost on the other.

Now when you're looking at revenue in a very simplistic form (assuming there is just one single product company), it is the multiplication of the market size, market share and price

On the cost side, there are three main costs:

1. First is the cost of acquiring a customer - you want a customer to come to your business (to your website or to your store), and for that you have to do some direct marketing and/or offer discounts. So the money spent in acquiring a new customer and making him do the first transaction is the Cost of acquisition (CAC)

2. Secondly, once a customer is already acquired, then you have to keep on sending some mailers, offer some incentives etc. to retain him and do subsequent transactions. This is the cost of retaining customers.

3. And thirdly the biggest cost is the cost of the manufacturing the product or delivering the service.

LTV is the **Life-time or Long-term value** of a customer is the margin that the business can generate from him or her as long as he or she continues to be the customer of the business. Let us understand this with an example:

1. Let us assume you run a startup of selling spectacles online through your website.

2. You run a google ad for Rs. 500 and acquire one customer only. The cost of acquisition or CAC is Rs. 500

3. Let us further assume that the margin your business earns on each sale of spectacles is Rs. 250.

4. There is historical data to suggest that each customers buys 4 spectacles from your website over a period of 2 years. The total margin that the customer gives your business is therefore Rs. 1000 (Rs. 250 *4). Rs. 1000, therefore, is the LTV of this customer

5. Comparing LTV of Rs. 1000 with a CAC of Rs. 500 shows that LTV/CAC ratio is 2 and therefore it's a profitable to acquire this customer. So if you have 100 customers, each one of us giving you 500 net margin, then eventually that means Rs. 50000 is the value that you have created for the business.

6. In the above example, the customer had to buy two spectacles to enable the startup to recover the CAC of Rs. 500. So till the time the customer does the second transaction, the startup has invested Rs. 250 in him or her (CAC of Rs. 500 minus the margin of the first transaction of Rs. 250). The best case is when the first transaction itself recover the CAC. In this

scenario, each transaction can generate a surplus which can be deployed in the business. In an education business, this is generally true.

This analysis of calculating the economics of a single transaction is called the "unit level economics". The margins from each transaction has not only to cover the variable cost but also the marketing expenses, product development expenses and corporate expenses.

Let's look at another practical aspect - When a business has just started, there is not enough data to calculate LTV as you do not have a customer who has lasted with the startup for two years or maybe because the startup has not been in the business for two years. How does one view LTV – CAC in this case or in other words, how does one take a call to spend CAC to acquire the customer? The answer is simple. You need two transactions from this customer in order to at least recover CAC. You take an informed view whether the customer will do at least two transactions or not. If the customer does the third transaction, it will create value for the business. But at least in two transactions, the value is not destroyed.

Customer Retention: Customer retention rate is the % of customers who continue to be your customers over a period of time e.g. if the customer retention rate is 70% after one year, it means that the 70% of the customers continue to be the startup customers after one year also. Startups have a retention strategy in place by offering discounts, loyalty benefits etc. and monitor the expenses attached with these activities. If the startup's product is heavily differentiated and solves a real pain point then the CAC is low as well the retaining cost is very low.

The three Contribution margins:
LTV- CAC analysis is done in conjunction with a set of three metrics – the 3 contribution margins. These three measurements or the three metrics investors routinely use to estimate the chance of a startup becoming a profitable a business in the future. This adds another layer of very useful information to the LTV- CAC analysis.

Let's look at the picture below.

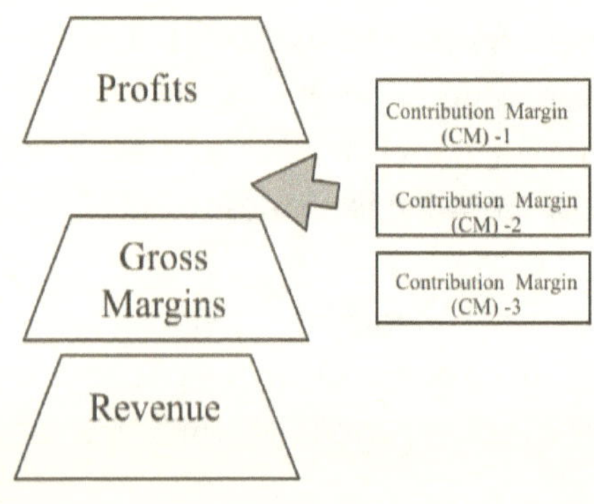

The eventual aim of the entire exercise is to estimate profits, since profits are not there or going to be there, we move one level below to estimate the Gross margin of the business. Gross margin is simply the revenue minus the variable cost. But to get profits from gross margins, there are several expenses that have to be taken out – the 3 contribution margins each have a different set of expenses taken out successively to get a directional sense on the long term viability of the business.

The following picture explains the definitions of the three contribute margins.

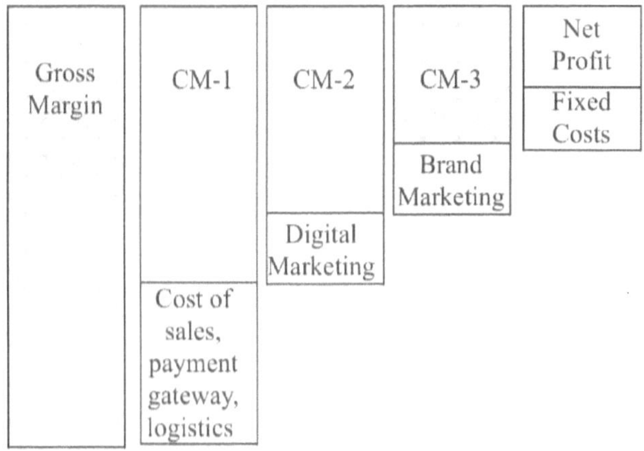

Each contribution margin shows a different path to profitability as the startup progresses from a startup to a mature company:

1. Revenue minus direct variable cost is the gross margin.

2. Now, if you take out the cost of sales, which is very basic cost of payment gateway, cost of logistics, cost of inventory, then what is left is contribution margin 1 (CM-1). Startups should be at least CM-1 positive.

3. If you take away the cost of acquiring a customer, that is the CAC from CM-1, you are left with CM- 2. Ideally speaking, CM- 2 should be positive because that indicates each transaction that the startup does with the customer is creating positive shareholder value. Each customer that the startup acquires gives a margin in the first transaction itself. When the startup scales up, the combined margin shall cover up all the other expenses such as R&D, corporate, marketing etc. One can also visualize the path to profitability. It gets into a positive value creation cycle.

4. CM-3 is CM- 2 minus brand marketing. Now brand marketing creates value over a period of time. Brand marketing is not going to give you any results in the early stages of the startup. CM-3 will almost always be negative and therefore if this is negative, the net profit which is basically

CM-3 minus fixed cost will be negative as well.

5. If an investor has to evaluate your startup to see how healthy your numbers are, how healthy your product differentiation is, how good you have targeted the customer segments, how efficiently you're using the channels, he's going to evaluate CM-1 and CM-2. As shown, ideally CM-2 should be positive. If CM-2 is not positive then at least CM-1 should be positive and LTV should be significantly more than CAC.

Now what is a burn rate? The burn rate refers to the rate at which a startup is spending its available cash to cover operational expenses. It is essentially the amount of money a startup is burning every month to survive. The "runway" refers to the number of months a startup can survive given its burn rate and its money in the bank. Ideally there should always be a runway of 9 months.

How to use the "unit economics" in practice:

A healthy LTV-CAC ratio is generally considered to be 3:1, meaning a customer should generate three times the revenue it costs to acquire him. If your ratio is below this, it's time to re-evaluate your business model or idea. If your product is already in the market, it's essential to figure out where you can improve this ratio. Otherwise, it might be prudent to abandon the idea and redirect your efforts elsewhere.

Analysis of contribution margin also helps you to determine units needed for breaking even the startup. Breakeven is the point where the startup can survive without depending on external capital.

The Path to Break-Even is the following:

1. Start with CM-1: Ensure your product generates value above its direct costs.

2. Optimize CM-2: Refine your marketing and sales strategy to achieve a sustainable CAC and boost LTV.

3. Aim for Positive CM-3: Plan for operational independence by aligning your break-even revenue with realistic milestones.

A founder has to continuously endeavor to make LTV-CAC ratio and unit economics more favorable:

1. Lowering Customer Acquisition Costs (CAC): Refine Your Targeting: Use data to identify your ideal customer segments and focus marketing efforts on them. Narrow targeting improves conversion rates and reduces wastage. An online learning platform may focus on students preparing for competitive exams rather than promoting to a general audience.

Invest in Organic Growth Channels: Rely less on paid advertising and more on sustainable channels like SEO, content marketing, and referrals. These channels have a higher upfront cost but result in lower long-term CAC. Zomato's early focus on user-generated content and local restaurant reviews created significant organic traffic, lowering its CAC over time.

Streamline the Sales Funnel: Simplify the customer journey. Ensure your website, app, or sales process is user-friendly, reducing drop-offs and improving conversion rates. E-commerce sites like Amazon use features like one-click checkout to streamline the buying process and improve CAC efficiency.

2. Increasing Lifetime Value (LTV): Enhance Retention Rates: Invest in post-purchase engagement strategies like loyalty programs, personalized emails, and excellent customer support. Loyal customers buy more frequently and stay longer. Flipkart's loyalty program, Flipkart Plus, encourages repeat purchases by offering free delivery and exclusive discounts.

Increase Cross-Sell and Upsell Opportunities: Offer complementary products or services that encourage customers to spend more. Razorpay upsells additional financial products like subscription billing or payroll solutions to its existing payment gateway clients.

Optimize Pricing: Reassess your pricing strategy. Even a small increase in pricing can significantly impact LTV without affecting demand if your product offers strong value.

3. Evaluate and Improve Contribution Margins: A deeper look at unit economics involves understanding your contribution margin, i.e., the revenue per unit minus variable costs. A positive contribution margin is critical for long-term success.

Reduce Variable Costs: Negotiate better terms with suppliers, optimize manufacturing, or streamline delivery processes. OYO improved contribution margins by standardizing its hotel operations and optimizing supply chain costs.

Focus on Higher-Margin Products: Prioritize products or services that yield higher margins. A SaaS startup might focus on selling annual subscriptions instead of monthly plans to improve cash flow and profitability.

4. Use Metrics for Iterative Improvement: Your LTV-CAC ratio and unit economics are not static. Regularly analyze and iterate to improve them:

• Monitor metrics like churn rate, customer acquisition sources, and campaign ROIs.

• Set benchmarks for your industry to understand where you stand.

• Create projections under different scenarios (e.g., best-case, worst-case).

Finally, if after significant efforts, the LTV-CAC ratio and unit economics remain unfavorable, it might be time to reconsider your business idea or model:

- Identify Bottlenecks: Is it a high CAC, low LTV, or both?
- Experiment with Changes: Try different customer segments, pricing strategies, or even product features to see what works.
- Know When to Let Go: Sometimes, the market dynamics or cost structures don't align. It's better to pivot than persist with an unsustainable model.

At the end of the day, building a startup isn't about checking off a list of buzzwords or chasing trends—it's about mastering the fundamentals that shape lasting businesses. Whether it's understanding your Total Addressable Market (TAM), finding your unique space in the profit pool, or creating an offering that differentiates itself along a real need, these are the pillars that determine success.

Equally important are the softer aspects: Can your idea be easily communicated and understood? Does your product inspire loyalty, making it habit-forming? And perhaps most crucially, do you have the discipline and clarity to execute in a way that ensures these building blocks work together seamlessly?

Eventually, all the frameworks, strategies, and metrics boil down to this: Do you solve a meaningful problem in a way that creates value for your customers while ensuring profitability for your business? If you focus on these essentials, you're already ahead of the curve.

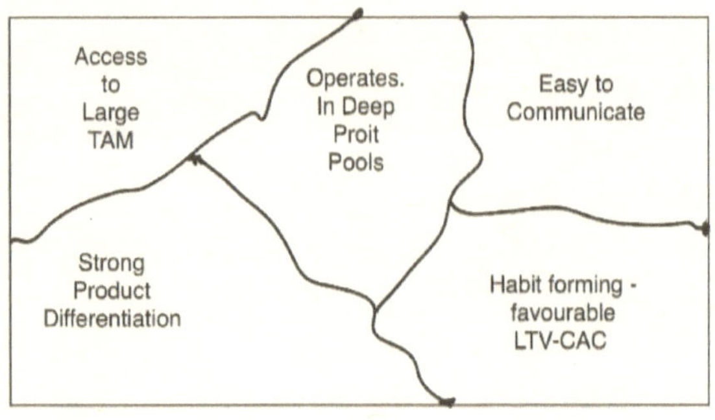

With the VIBE framework, you've built a strong foundation for your startup—one that is rooted in a well-validated idea, clear unit economics, and a deep understanding of your market. Now, it's time to shift focus to practical tools and strategies that will support the startup's journey forward.

This final section of the book dives into the essential preparation every founder needs to be carry out at the time of formation of the startup.

Part 4: Practical Guidelines on the VC process

Introduction: Part 4

Not all startups need VC funds. But if you do, the objective of this stage is to get you ready to face the expectations of investors.

Here's what is covered in the last part of the book:

1. Planning Your Startup's Funding Requirements
2. Valuation
3. Approaching the Funding Journey
4. Crafting Your Pitch Deck
5. Building a Financial Model

Chapter 8: Planning Your Startup's Funding Requirements

A crucial part of building a startup is determining how much funding you need—and when you need it. Securing all the money upfront may seem like a dream scenario, but it's often impractical and counterproductive. Startups evolve, and both founders and investors prefer to commit funds in phases. This approach ensures capital is allocated efficiently while progress is made at each stage.

Why Funding is Phased:

1. Efficient Use of Resources: Having too much money early on can lead to wasteful spending. Phased funding forces startups to stay disciplined and focused on achieving milestones.

2. Risk Mitigation for Investors: Investors want to see measurable progress before committing larger amounts. By funding in stages, they reduce their exposure to risk while ensuring your startup is on the right track.

3. Valuation Growth: As your startup achieves milestones, its valuation increases. Raising funds at a higher valuation in later stages reduces dilution for founders.

The Importance of Maintaining Runway:

Runway refers to the amount of time your startup can operate before running out of money. Always plan for a runway of at least 9 to 12 months; here's why:

1. Buffer for Fundraising: Raising funds takes time. The fundraising process itself can take up to 6 months or more, so your runway ensures you're not caught off guard.

2. Operational Stability: A longer runway allows you to execute your plans without constant fear of running out of resources, which can distract from growth.

When calculating your funding requirements, ensure that your burn rate (monthly expenses) aligns with maintaining this runway at all times.

Breaking Down Your Funding Requirements:

When estimating your funding needs, divide them into phases based on the startup lifecycle. Here's a step-by-step approach:

1. Define Key Milestones for Each Phase: Funding should align with the goals you aim to achieve in each stage.

- Pre-seed/Seed Stage: Idea validation, building an MVP (Minimum Viable Product), and initial customer acquisition.
- Series A: Scaling the product, expanding the team, and increasing market reach.

- Series B and Beyond: Optimizing operations, entering new markets, and growing revenue.

2. Estimate Costs for Each Milestone: Break down your funding requirements into categories such as:
- Product Development: Costs for building or refining your product.
- Team Salaries: Hiring talent essential to your growth.
- Marketing and Customer Acquisition: Budgets for campaigns, ads, or promotional activities.
- Operational Expenses: Office space, technology tools, and other infrastructure.

Example: If your goal in the seed stage is to acquire 10,000 users, estimate costs for product development, marketing, and operational needs to hit that milestone.

3. **Include a Buffer:** Always factor in a 10–20% buffer for unexpected expenses. Startups rarely follow linear paths, and this cushion can help navigate unforeseen challenges.

As your startup progresses, your understanding of the market, customers, and challenges evolves. Use this information to:
- Reassess your milestones and adjust funding needs accordingly.

- Prepare a clear funding plan for investors that explains how their capital will be used and what outcomes they can expect.

4. **Raise to Hit the Next Milestone**: Funding should align with tangible goals, such as launching an MVP, achieving user growth, or generating revenue. These milestones validate your business and make it easier to secure the next round at a higher valuation.

Investors typically take 10–20% equity at each funding stage. This ensures founders retain control while providing investors a meaningful stake. Example:
- Seed Stage: You raise $1 m for 15% equity, valuing your startup at $6.7 m post-money.
- Series A: You raise $5 m again offering 15% equity, increasing the valuation to $33.3 m.

This balance ensures sufficient funding without excessive dilution, preserving founder incentives.

The Two Full-Time Jobs of a Founder

Being a founder means wearing multiple hats, but two responsibilities stand out as full-time roles:

1. Building and Running the Business: This involves creating the product, growing the team,

acquiring customers, and ensuring day-to-day operations run smoothly.

2. Raising Funds: Fundraising is a continuous process. Even after one round is closed, founders must start preparing for the next, keeping investor relationships warm, refining the pitch, and tracking key metrics to showcase progress.

The ability to balance these two roles is what sets successful founders apart. Neglecting either can stall the business or jeopardize its financial stability. Founders must at all times:

• Track Metrics: Consistently monitor KPIs like revenue, burn rate, and runway to demonstrate progress.

• Maintain Investor Relationships: Keep current and potential investors updated on milestones and challenges.

• Refine the Pitch: Adapt your story as your startup evolves, incorporating feedback from each round.

Founders who proactively approach fundraising are better positioned to secure capital under favorable terms and avoid last-minute desperation. If required, they should seek inputs from experienced founders or mentors to refine their funding strategy.

Chapter 9: Valuation

In the context of this book, the primary focus is to help you generate, refine, and validate your startup ideas. However, for the sake of completeness, it is essential to briefly address the topic of valuation—a crucial aspect of the entrepreneurial journey.

1. The Nature of Early-Stage Valuation

Valuation at the early stages of a startup is more of an art than a science. Unlike mature companies with stable revenues and clear financial projections, early-stage startups often lack the data required for traditional valuation methods. If we were to adhere strictly to financial principles, the value of an unproven idea might be considered negligible. However, the reality is far more nuanced.

A key consideration is the opportunity cost borne by the founder. As a startup founder, you may be leaving behind a stable career, a steady income, and a sense of security. This sacrifice— alongside your vision and the potential for transformative impact—forms the basis for early-stage valuations.

2. Reverse Calculation by Investors

In early-stage funding, investors often reverse-engineer valuations based on the percentage of equity they require to justify their risk and achieve desired returns. For example, if an investor needs a 10x return on a $500,000 investment, they might demand a stake to align with the startup's projected growth trajectory.

This reverse calculation is inherently tied to the perceived potential of your idea, the team's capabilities, and prevailing market trends.

3. Market Benchmarks and Sector Trends

Early-stage valuations are heavily influenced by sector-specific benchmarks and market sentiment at the time of funding. For instance:

- Hot Sectors: Startups in trending industries, such as AI or renewable energy, may command higher valuations even with minimal traction.

- Geographic Influence: Valuations may also vary by region. For example, a startup in Silicon Valley might secure a higher valuation than a similar one in a smaller ecosystem.

4. Mid-Stage and Later-Stage Valuations

As your startup progresses, valuation becomes less abstract and more data-driven. With revenue figures, user growth metrics, and operational data, investors can benchmark your performance against:

- Listed Comparables: Public companies in the same industry provide valuation multiples,

such as price-to-sales (P/S) or price-to-earnings (P/E) ratios.

- Transaction Comparables: Valuations from recent funding rounds or acquisitions in your sector help establish a baseline.

For instance, a SaaS startup generating $2 million in annual recurring revenue (ARR) might be valued at a multiple of 10x ARR, based on industry standards.

5. The Role of Term Sheets and Shareholder Rights: Early-stage investors often negotiate term sheets that include specific rights to protect their investments. These might include:

- Liquidation Preferences: Ensuring investors recoup their investment before other stakeholders in case of liquidation.
- Anti-Dilution Clauses: Protecting the investor's ownership percentage in future rounds.
- Board Seats: Providing strategic oversight and influence over key decisions.

While these terms may seem restrictive, they are designed to align the interests of founders and investors, fostering mutual success.

Key Takeaways for Founders:

1. Understand Opportunity Cost: Your valuation reflects not only your idea but also the personal and financial sacrifices you're making as a founder.

2. Leverage Sector Trends: Stay informed about valuation benchmarks in your industry and region to negotiate effectively.

3. Prepare for Negotiation: Early-stage valuation is often a negotiation based on perception, potential, and market dynamics.

4. Focus on Milestones: Demonstrating clear progress and achieving key milestones can significantly boost your valuation in subsequent funding rounds.

5. Balance Equity and Control: While securing funding is important, consider the long-term implications of equity dilution and shareholder rights.

Valuation is an evolving aspect of the startup journey, starting as an abstract negotiation and becoming increasingly data-driven as your business grows. By understanding the dynamics at each stage, founders can approach valuation with confidence, aligning their goals with those of their investors. Whether you're raising your first seed round or preparing for Series A, the key is to focus on building a compelling business that justifies its worth in the eyes of your investors.

Chapter 10: Approaching the Funding Journey

Securing funding is one of the most critical, challenging and fulfilling tasks for any entrepreneur. The journey typically unfolds in stages, aligning with the growth of the business. In the very beginning, startups often rely on *friends and family*—those who believe in the founder's vision, even when there's little more than an idea to show. This early support is vital, as traditional funding sources like banks rarely invest in startups due to their lack of collateral and high risk.

The next step often involves reaching out to *angel investors*. These are typically affluent individuals willing to back startups during their early days. They provide not only funding but also mentorship, connections, and advice. Platforms like AngelList and LetsVenture make it easier for founders to connect with angel investors and syndicates, democratizing access to capital. For startups looking for additional structure and guidance, pre-accelerators and accelerators like Y Combinator or Techstars or asisa.vc can be invaluable. These programs combine seed funding with mentorship, workshops, and networking opportunities, significantly improving a startup's chances of success.

Once a startup demonstrates traction - whether through user growth, product-market fit, or revenue - venture capital (VC) becomes the natural next step. VCs bring in larger pools of money, typically investing at the seed stage or in growth-stage rounds (Series A and beyond). Founders often approach VCs directly, leveraging warm introductions through mutual contacts or personalized pitches. Alternatively, for larger or more complex funding rounds, startups may engage investment bankers who specialize in deal structuring and investor matchmaking. Many of these bankers are sector specialists as well.

The approach to funding evolves with your startup's growth. In the early stages, it's about leveraging your personal network and smaller, focused groups like angels and accelerators. As the stakes grow, the ecosystem widens to include institutional players like VCs and later-stage investors. Knowing when and how to approach the right investors is as much an art as it is a science—and mastering it can define the trajectory of your startup.

The venture capital ecosystem has become the cornerstone of innovation, driving industries forward and enabling the global success of startups.

Chapter 11: Crafting Your Pitch Deck

The fundamental objective of any pitch deck is to convince the investors on the following questions:

1. The founders have found this genuine pain point which impacts a large number of people

2. The opportunity is big and the founders have a solution

     i. Enough people will pay for this solution to that problem

     ii. That price is good for the startup to make money

     iii. The solution cannot be easily copied

3. The founders have done substantial research and work

4. The founders are the right experienced team to do all this

5. The investors will not be cheated by the startup or its founders

The challenges that a startup faces:
- A VC firm will typically sit through 10-15 pitches in a day. So how do a startup stand out in a sea of startups clamoring for attention?
- Once a VC firms passes an investment opportunity, it's very unlikely that they will revisit it soon - for the founders, it's a lost opportunity if the pitch was not up to the mark.

- The deck should be self-contained and complete if someone wants to read through it in the absence of founders
- The most successful pitch decks weave a compelling narrative, one that paints a vivid picture of the problem, the solution, and the world that awaits on the other side of their innovation. It's about making investors feel and imagine, not just think.

To cover the above points, following are the elements of a strong narrative or a pitch deck:

Problem Statement	Begin with a strong hook to grab attention. This could be a compelling statistic, an intriguing question, or a powerful statement that highlights the problem your product or service solves. Elaborate by breaking down the problem into elements (utilizing The Idea Shaker Framework) demonstrating your deep understanding.
Solution and Market Size	Give a real example of how your product helped an early customer, if possible. Expand from that customer to the

	larger customer base and mention the market size. Provide summary data only (details and calculations in the annexure).
Competition	The investor is thinking about the competition now. Present a chart for comparisons honestly highlighting the differences. If possible, carry the products to showcase the differentiation.
Showcase the Traction	Showcase any traction or milestones achieved to date. This could include customer testimonials, user growth metrics, revenue figures, partnerships, or any other evidence of progress. Traction helps validate your business and reduces investor risk.
The "founders"	The objective here is to convey that the founders are uniquely positioned to do this. Showcase what you have left behind to do this startup- your opportunity cost. Highlight if

	you are already signed a "founders' agreement". Speak about: • Industry experience • Fund raising • Team building and management experience in any role.
The Plan	Share top level numbers, unit level economics, market share projections etc. if possible. Give examples from your experience why these seem reasonable.
The Team	Talk about the early hires and their background. Share the ESOP plan, if already in place
Corporate governance	Highlight the background and credibility of the advisory team, the independent directors, and the auditor etc. - whatever you can do to give comfort even if it's not being explicitly asked.

Chapter 12: Building a Financial Model

Creating a financial model for an early-stage startup is a blend of art and science. It's less about precise forecasts and more about presenting a clear, thoughtful roadmap that demonstrates the startup's potential, its funding needs, and how it will allocate resources to achieve growth. Here's how to craft a robust financial model:

1. Start with the Basics

The financial model should begin with a clear overview of the business's revenue streams and cost structure. This sets the foundation for understanding how money flows in and out of the startup.

For revenue streams, identify all potential sources of income. For example, a SaaS company might rely on subscription fees, while an e-commerce platform could include product sales and advertising revenue. Break these down into monthly or quarterly figures based on your expected customer acquisition and pricing strategy.

On the cost side, distinguish between fixed costs (e.g., office rent, employee salaries) and variable costs (e.g., production costs, delivery fees). Fixed costs remain constant regardless of scale, while variable costs increase with higher sales volumes. This distinction is vital to understanding how scaling will impact profitability.

2. Focus on Unit Economics

As has been covered in the VIBE Framework, Unit economics is the cornerstone of financial modeling for early-stage startups. It assesses the profitability of selling a single unit of your product or service, providing insights into whether the business model is scalable. Calculate CM-1, CM-2 and CM-3 to the extent possible given the lack of data and history of the startup.

3. Map-out the Next 6 Quarters

Early-stage startups need to focus on short-term milestones – making hypothetical projections for the next five years adds no value to the investor except estimating a top line revenue and market share that can be achieved in years 3 and 5. Creating a financial projection for the next six quarters helps founders and investors visualize how the business will evolve.

Start with revenue projections, breaking them down by expected customer growth and pricing. For costs, account for both fixed and variable expenses, showing how they will change as the business scales.

Also, calculate the burn rate—the amount of cash your startup spends each month—and the resulting runway, or how long your current cash reserves will last.

4. Funding Requirements and Allocation

A financial model should clearly state the startup's funding needs and how the funds will be used. Divide the funding into key categories, such as team expansion, marketing, technology development, and working capital. For example:
- ₹50 lakhs for marketing to acquire 10,000 users over the next six months.
- ₹30 lakhs for technology development to enhance scalability and user experience.

Clearly link these allocations to business milestones, such as achieving a specific revenue target or acquiring a defined number of customers.

5. Incorporate Scenarios

Given the uncertainty in early-stage startups, build best-case, base-case, and worst-case scenarios into your financial model. These scenarios can help identify risks and prepare mitigation strategies.

For instance, in the worst-case scenario, customer acquisition might be slower than expected, increasing the time required to reach breakeven. This would necessitate additional funding or cost adjustments.

6. Keep It Simple and Visual

A financial model is most effective when it's easy to understand. Use tables, charts, and graphs to present your projections visually. For example:

- A bar graph comparing projected revenues and costs across quarters.
- A pie chart showing the allocation of funding across different areas.

7. Add Industry-Specific Metrics

Depending on your industry, include metrics that provide deeper insights. For example:

- SaaS Startups: Monthly Recurring Revenue (MRR), Churn Rate.
- E-commerce Startups: Average Order Value (AOV), Customer Retention Rate.
- Consumer Startups: Active Users, Daily Engagement Metrics.

These metrics showcase your understanding of the business and its unique challenges.

8. Profitability Milestones

Outline when and how the business will reach profitability. This doesn't mean you need to show immediate profits—most early-stage startups don't. However, investors want to see a clear path to positive unit economics and, eventually, overall profitability. Highlight key milestones, such as:

- Achieving breakeven at a specific customer base

- Scaling revenue to cover fixed costs
- Reducing CAC through optimized marketing strategies

A financial model for an early-stage startup is a living document that evolves as your business grows. Its primary goal is to help founders and investors understand the startup's trajectory, funding needs, and scalability potential.

Notes

Notes

Notes